# The Cambridge English Course

**1**

**Student's Book**

Michael Swan and Catherine Walter

Cambridge University Press

Cambridge    London    New York    New Rochelle    Melbourne    Sydney

...4.
...as printed
...d continuously
...ince 1584.

...by the Press Syndicate of the University of Cambridge
...t Building, Trumpington Street, Cambridge CB2 1RP
...East 57th Street, New York, NY10022, USA
10 Stamford Road, Oakleigh, Melbourne 3166, Australia

© Cambridge University Press 1984

First published 1984
Ninth printing 1987

Designed by John Youé and Associates, Croydon, Surrey
Typeset by Text Filmsetters Limited, London
Origination by Vyner Litho Plates Limited, London
Printed in Great Britain by Blantyre Printing and Binding, Glasgow

ISBN 0 521 28908 4  Student's Book 1
Split edition: ISBN 0 521 31028 8  Part A
              ISBN 0 521 31029 6  Part B
              ISBN 0 521 31030 X  Part C

ISBN 0 521 28909 2  Practice Book 1
ISBN 0 521 28910 6  Teacher's Book 1
ISBN 0 521 27865 1  Test Book 1
ISBN 0 521 24703 9  Cassette Set 1
ISBN 0 521 26223 2  Student's Cassette 1

## Author's acknowledgements

A book like this necessarily owes a great deal to a great many people. Our thanks to:

Alan Maley, for the splendid seminar programme which he organized at the British Council, Paris, in the 1970s. This was an unparalleled source of information, ideas and inspiration.

Donn Byrne, Alan Duff, Alan Maley, Heather Murray, Penny Ur and Jane Wright, for specific ideas and exercises which we have borrowed.

The many other people — too many to acknowledge — whose ideas have influenced our work, including all the colleagues and students from whom we have learnt.

Those institutions and teachers who were kind enough to work with the Pilot Edition of this course, and whose comments have done so much to shape the final version. (A full list of the institutions involved is given on the Acknowledgements page.)

Peter Roach and Ian Thompson for their expert and sensible help with the phonetic transcription.

John Youé, Steve Williams, Gillian Clack, Richard Child, Chris Rawlings, Clifford Webb and Diana Dobson of Youé and Spooner Limited, our designers, for their unfailing understanding, good humour and expertise.

John and Angela Eckersley, and the staff of the Eckersley School of English, Oxford, for making it possible for us to try out parts of the book in their classrooms.

Steve Dixon, Lorna Higgs, John Peake, Pat Robbins, Fran Searson, Ann Swan, Ruth Swan, Heather and Paul Teale, Sue Ward, Adrian Webber, and Susan Webber, for agreeing to be quizzed and questioned within earshot of our microphones.

Judy Haycox, Joanne Haycox, Susan Webber and Helen Walter, for invaluable domestic support during a trying period.

Mark, for patience and good humour beyond the call of duty.

And finally, to Adrian du Plessis, Peter Donovan, Barbara Thomas and Peter Ducker of Cambridge University Press: few authors can have been so fortunate in their publishers.

Michael Swan    Catherine Walter

# Contents

# Map of Book 1*

| In Unit | Students will learn to | Students will learn to talk about |
|---|---|---|
| 1 | Ask and give names; say hello; ask and tell where people are from. | Numbers. |
| 2 | Say hello formally and informally; ask about and give personal information. | Jobs; age. |
| 3 | Describe people; tell the time. | Family relationships. |
| 4 | Describe places; give compliments; express uncertainty; confirm and correct information. | Geography; numbers to 1,000,000. |
| 5 | Describe houses and flats; make and answer telephone calls. | Home: furniture, addresses; telephones. |
| 6 | Express likes and dislikes; ask about and describe habits and routines. | Habits and routines. |
| 7 | Ask and tell about quantity. | Food and drink; shopping; quantification. |
| 8 | Ask for and give directions; ask and tell about physical and emotional states. | Finding your way in a town. |
| 9 | Express degrees of certainty; talk about frequency. | How people live; how animals live; weather and climate. |
| 10 | Describe people's appearances; give compliments; write simple letters. | Colours; parts of the body; clothing; resemblances. |
| 11 REVISION | Use what they have learnt in different ways. | Physical description. |
| 12 | Ask for and give information. | Personal history: differences between past and present; recent past. |
| 13 | Make and grant requests; say where things are; check information. | Shopping; travelling. |
| 14 | Ask for and give information. | Abilities; comparison; similarities and differences. |
| 15 | Ask for and give information; narrate. | Change; history. |
| 16 | Ask for and give opinions; agree and disagree; ask follow-up questions. | Weights and measures; appearances; professions; personality types; dates. |
| 17 | Order meals; make and reply to requests; borrow; make and reply to offers. | Food; restaurants; differences in formality; having guests at home. |
| 18 | Express guesses; write postcards. | Temporary present actions and states; holidays; change; economics and demography. |
| 19 | Plan; make, accept and decline invitations and suggestions. | Travel; distance; going out. |
| 20 | Initiate conversations, express interest; ask for, express and react to opinions. | Meeting strangers; frequency; likes and dislikes; being in love; duration. |
| 21 | Ask for and give reasons. | Physical qualities; composition of objects; personal possessions; production; imports and exports. |
| 22 REVISION | Describe; ask for and give personal information; use what they have learnt in different ways. | Comparison; shopping; people's appearance and behaviour. |
| 23 | Give instructions and advice. | Sports; position, direction and change of position; cooking. |
| 24 | Make requests; ask for and give information. | Hotels; public transport; air travel; place and direction. |
| 25 | Talk about plans; make predictions. | Plans; small ads; travel. |
| 26 | Talk about problems; express sympathy; make suggestions; express and respond to emotions; describe relationships. | Common physical problems; personal relationships. |
| 27 | Narrate. | Ways of travelling; speed; how things are done. |
| 28 | Describe objects; narrate. | Education systems; quantity; shapes; parts of things; position; structuring of time-sequences; daily routines. |
| 29 | Predict; warn; raise and counter objections. | Danger; horoscopes. |
| 30 | Classify; make and accept apologies; correct misunderstandings; complain. | Need; importance; use and usefulness; shopping. |
| 31 | Make, accept and decline offers; ask for and analyse information. | Reciprocal and reflexive action; self and others; social situations; possession. |
| 32 REVISION | Express obligation and opinions; other functions dependent on your choice of activities. | Correctness; other areas depending on activities chosen. |

*This 'map' of the course should be translated into the students' language where possible.

4

VOCABULARY: Students will learn about 1100 common words and expressions during the course.

| Students will learn these grammar points | Students will study these aspects of pronunciation |
|---|---|
| Present of *to be* (singular); possessive adjectives. | Word-stress; weak forms. |
| *A/an* with jobs; subject pronouns. | Rhythm; intonation; linking; stress pattern recognition. |
| Noun plurals; *'s* for possession; present of *to be* (plural); *have got*; adjectives; adverbs of degree. | /ð/; *o* in *mother*, etc.; stress; intonation; linking /r/. |
| *A/an* contrasted with *the*; adjectives before nouns; *on/in/at* with places; *Isn't that...?* | /θ/ and /ð/; /ðə/ and /ði:/; word-stress and resultant /ə/; intonation of answers; intonation for contrast; linking. |
| *There is/there are*; simple present affirmative, *this/that*; *Can/Could I...?*; *tell* + object + *that*-clause; formation of noun plurals. | Weak forms; linking and rhythm with *there is/there are*; contrastive stress; rising and falling intonation; plural endings. |
| Simple Present; omission of article; *like* + *-ing*; *neither...nor*; object pronouns; *at* with times; *by* (*bus*); *from...until*. | Stress and rhythm; decoding fast speech. |
| Countables and uncountables; expressions of quantity; omission of article; *was/were*; *some* and *any*; *much* and *many*. | Word-stress; weak forms. |
| *For* + expressions of distance; *to be* with *hungry, thirsty*, etc. | Intonation of polite questions; stress and rhythm; weak form of *at*. |
| Complex sentences; text building; frequency adverbs; impersonal *it*. | Stress and /ə/; /i:/ and /ɪ/. |
| *Have got*; *both* and *all*; *look like*; *What (a)...!* | |
| (Revision) *Be* contrasted with *have*; *there is/there are*; questions with noun-phrase subjects. | Perceiving weak forms and unstressed words; /θ/ and /ð/; intonation; pronunciation of words with misleading spellings. |
| Simple Past; *do* as pro-verb; subject and object questions with *who*. | Regular Simple Past endings; stress in negative sentences; rhythm and stress in questions. |
| *One(s)* as substitute word; *would like*; *much* and *many*. | Rising intonation in *yes/no* questions; falling intonation in answers; rhythm. |
| *Can*; *good at* + noun/*-ing* word; comparative and superlative of adjectives; *a bit/much* + adjective. | /kn/, /kæn/, /kɑ:nt/; pronunciations of the letter *a*, weak forms of *as* and *from*. |
| *Ago*; *a* contrasted with *the*; past of *to be*; Simple Past; sequencing devices. | Linking; strong and weak forms of *was* and *were*; rhythm. |
| *Be* with ages and measures; *look like/be like*; dates; *with* for possession; *a/any*. | /θ/; pronunciations of the letter *i*. |
| *A little/a few*; *I'll have*; *Could you...?*; *give/bring/lend/show* + two objects, object pronouns; indirect object with *to*; *something to eat/drink*. | Politeness through intonation; pronunciations of the letter *o*. |
| Present Progressive; *the girl in jeans*; *the man with a beard*; *get* + comparative; spelling *-ing* forms; contrast of two present tenses. | Pronunciations of the letter *e*. |
| Present Progressive with future meaning; coordination with *so*; *each* + singular; *who* as object; *How far is ... from ...?*; *Let's*; *Why don't we...?* | Pronunciations of the letter *u*; decoding fast colloquial speech. |
| *Do you mind if...?*; reply questions; adverbs and adverbials of frequency; *So do/can/am/have I*; Present Perfect; *since* and *for*. | /i:/ and /ɪ/. |
| *Why* + negative verb; *too* + adjective; adjective + *enough*; *made of*; Simple Past and Present Perfect; Passives; relative *which*; *to* and *from*. | Linking final consonants to initial vowels; linking between adjacent vowels. |
| (Revision) *more...than*; *as...as*; *not as...as*; *less...than*; (*not*) *the same as*; *different from*; *but*; revision of tenses. | |
| Imperatives; *if*-clauses; prepositions of place and movement; *should* + infinitive; grammar of written and spoken instructions. | Letter *o* pronounced /ɒ/ and /ʌ/. |
| *Have to*; infinitive of purpose; preposition + *-ing* form; prepositions of place and direction. | Devoicing of /v/ in *have to*. |
| *Going to*; connectors in paragraphs; paragraph-structuring adverbials; infinitives and *-ing* forms. | Spellings of /ɜ:/; pronunciation of *going to*. |
| *It* + Simple Present + *me*; *It makes me* + adjective. | 'Long' and 'short' vowels. |
| Superlatives; different meanings of *get*; adverbs of manner; adjectives and adverbs. | Decoding fast speech. |
| Quantifying expressions; fractions; *at the top/bottom* etc.; *in* and *at* for time; structuring with adverbs and conjunctions. | Identifying unstressed words; word-stress and /ə/. |
| *Will* + infinitive; *get lost/killed/married*. | Pronunciation of *w, 'll, won't*. |
| *X uses y to do z* (*with*); *x does y with z*; words having more than one grammatical function. | Use of stress for emphasis and contrast. |
| Reflexive/emphatic pronouns; *each other*; *somebody else*; *Shall I...?*; *I'd love/prefer/like*; *to* as pro-verb; *whose*; *somebody/anybody* etc. | Strong and weak pronunciations of *shall*; decoding unstressed words in fast speech. |
| (Revision) *have to*; *should*; verb tenses; question forms; adjectives; and other structures dependent on students' choice of activities. | |

# Hello

## A What's your name?

1. ....................

2. ....................

3. ....................

4. ....................

5. ....................

6. ....................

7. ....................

8. ....................

9. ....................

10. ....................

## 1
1. Listen to the conversations.
2. Put the sentences into the pictures.

| |
|---|
| What's your name?    Hello. My name's Mary Lake.<br>No, it isn't.    Catherine.<br>Hello. Yes, room three four six, Mrs Lake.<br>What's *your* name?    Is your name Mark Perkins?<br>John.    Thank you.    It's Harry Brown. |

## 2 Say your name.

'Hello. My name's ..............'

## 3 Ask other students' names.

'What's your name?'

## 4 Ask and answer.

'Is your name Anne?' 'Yes, it is.'
'Is your name Alex?' 'No, it isn't. It's Peter.'

## 5 Pronunciation. Say these words and expressions after the recording.

what   what's   your   my   name   it
it's   isn't
Yes, it is.    No, it isn't.

## 6 Learn:

| | | | | |
|---|---|---|---|---|
| 1 one | 2 two | 3 three | 4 four | 5 five |
| 6 six | 7 seven | 8 eight | 9 nine | 10 ten |

# B His name's Robert Redford

**1** Put the right first names with the right surnames.

| First names: | Paul | Sebastian | Billie Jean |
| Jacqueline | Karel | Robert | James | Indira |
| Jane | Brigitte |

**Surnames:** Wojtila   Bond   Fonda McCartney   King   Onassis   Coe   Bardot Ghandi   Redford

**2** Put the right names with the photos.

1. His name's Paul McCartney.'

**3** Write sentences. Examples:

1. His first name is Paul
1. His surname is McCartney
4. Her name is Jane Fonda

**4** Ask about other students.

'What's his surname?' 'I don't know.'
'Is her first name Anne?' 'Yes, that's right.'
'Is her name Barbara?' 'No, it isn't.'

ABCDEFGHIJKLMNOPQRSTUVWXYZ
abcdefghijklmnopqrstuvwxyz

**5** Listen to these letters and practise saying them.

BCDGPTV   HQRWYZ   AEIOU
FLMNSX   JK

**6** Listen and write the words.

name   go......   h......   r......

**7** Spell your name.

# C How are you?

## 1 Listen, and practise the conversation.

## 2 Close your books. Can you remember the conversation?

## 3 Listen to the recording and complete the conversations.

ALICE: Excuse me. ........... ........... ...........
Fred Andrews?
JAKE: ..........., I'm sorry, ........... ........... It's
Jake Barker.
ALICE: ........... sorry.

ALICE: Excuse me. Are ........... Fred Andrews?
FRED: ..........., I am.
ALICE: Oh, ........... . ........... Alice Watson.
FRED: Oh, yes. How do you do?
ALICE: ........... ........... ........... ...........?

## 4 Practise the conversations.

## 5 Listen to the recording and answer.

## 6 Say these numbers.

1 6 3 4 8 9 2 7 5 10

## 7 Learn these numbers.

11 eleven   12 twelve   13 thirteen   14 fourteen   15 fifteen   16 sixteen   17 seventeen
18 eighteen   19 nineteen   20 twenty

# D Where are you from?

France        Scotland
Russia        The United States
England       Poland
India         Italy

## 1 Where's he from? Where's she from?

He's from ............        She's from ............

............        ............        ............

............        ............

## 2 Ask and answer.

I'm from India.

Where are you from?

I'm from Paris.

## 3 Use your dictionary.

| COUNTRY | NATIONALITY |
|---|---|
| Carla's from Italy. | She's Italian. |
| Erik's from Germany. | He's German. |
| Shu-fang's from China. | He's ............ |
| Rob's from ............ | He's Australian. |
| Helena's from Greece. | She's ............ |
| Kenji's from ............ | He's Japanese. |
| Joyce is from the United States. | She's American. |
| Andrew's from ............ | He's Scottish. |
| Colette's from Switzerland. | She's ............ |
| Steve's from Britain. | He's ............ |

## 4

My name's Susie. I'm from Switzerland. I speak German, French and a little English. And you?

## 5 Pronunciation: stress. Listen and repeat.

☐☐    ☐☐☐    ☐☐
**Eng**land    **It**aly    Ja**pan**
**Eng**lish    **Ger**many    Chi**nese**
**Brit**ain    **Swit**zerland
**Brit**ish    ☐☐☐
**Ger**man    Japa**nese**    I**tal**ian
**Chi**na        A**mer**ican
            Aus**tral**ian

## 6
1. Listen, and write the numbers.
2. Listen, and write the letters.

## 7 Look at the summary on page 134 with your teacher.

# Jobs

## A What do you do?

doctor   secretary   electrician
housewife   shop assistant   artist

**1** Complete the sentences.

1. He's an *artist*.

2. He's a ............

3. She's a ............

4. She's a ............

5. He's an ............

6. She's a ............

**2** Say what you do.

'I'm an engineer.'
'I'm a medical student.'
'I'm a photographer.'
'I'm between jobs.'

**3** Ask and answer.

A: *What do you do?*
B: *I'm a dentist.*
C: *I'm an artist.*
D: *I'm a housewife.*

**4** Say what other students do.

'She's a doctor.'
'He's an electrician.'

**5** Pronunciation. Listen and practise.

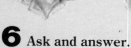

What do you do?

I'm a secretary.

Are you a doctor?

No, I'm an artist. She's a doctor.

Are you a photographer?

Yes, I am. Are you an artist?

No, I'm not. I'm a doctor. He's an artist.

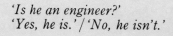

**6** Ask and answer.

'Are you a doctor?'
'Yes, I am.' / 'No, I'm not.'

'Is she an artist?'
'Yes, she is.' / 'No, she isn't.'

'Is he an engineer?'
'Yes, he is.' / 'No, he isn't.'

# B  I'm an actress. And you?

## 1 Listening for information. Listen, and complete the table.

| NAME | NATIONALITY | OCCUPATION | MARRIED/SINGLE |
|------|-------------|------------|----------------|
| Bill | | | don't know |
| Lucy | | | married |
| John Webb | | | |
| Gérard | French | | |
| Annie | | Photographer | |
| Philip | | | |

## 2 Which word is different?

. doctor (name) artist secretary
. her my he your
. from two four seven
. Britain France Germany Mary
. are is not am
. Excuse Russian Chinese Italian

## 3 Which stress? Listen and decide.

thirty Canada engineer married chemist
Hello thirteen Chinese Japanese
secretary doctor Goodbye

□□   □□   □□□   □□□

.Hello...   ..........   ..........   ..........

## 4 Complete the dialogue and practise it.

VIRGINIA: Hello, I'm Virginia. What's your name?
YOU: ............................................
VIRGINIA: Is that an English name?
YOU: ............................................
............................................?
VIRGINIA: No, I'm not. I'm Argentinian.
YOU: ............................., Virginia?
VIRGINIA: I'm an actress. And you?
YOU: ............................................
VIRGINIA: That's interesting. Are you married?
YOU: ............................................
............................................?
VIRGINIA: Yes, I am.

. Think of a person

OR cut a picture
out of a magazine.

2. Write about the person.

# C I'm very well, thank you

morning

afternoon

evening

night

## 1 Morning, afternoon, evening or night? Example: *1.* *morning or night*

## 2 Listen. Learn the new words from a dictionary or from your teacher. Listen again and practise.

WOMAN: Good morning, Mr Roberts. How are you?
MAN: Oh, good morning, Dr Wagner. I'm very well, thank you. And you?
WOMAN: I'm fine, thank you.

MAN: Hello, Mary.
WOMAN: Hi, Tom. How are you?
MAN: Fine, thanks. And you?
WOMAN: Not bad – but my daughter's not well today.
MAN: Oh, I'm sorry to hear that.

## 3 *Good morning* or *Hello*?

## 4 Differences. Read the conversations again and complete the table.

| Conversation 1 | Conversation 2 |
|---|---|
| 1. *Good morning* | Hello/Hi |
| 2. ............................ | Mary |
| 3. *How are you?* | How are you? |
| 4. ............................ | Fine/Not bad |
| 5. ............................ | thanks |
| 6. ............................ | And you? |

## 5 Stand up, walk around if you can, and greet other students.

# D How old are you?

## 1 Listen and practise.

| | | |
|---|---|---|
| 20 twenty | 30 thirty | 40 forty |
| 21 twenty-one | 34 thirty-four | 50 fifty |
| 22 twenty-two | 35 thirty-five | 60 sixty |
| 23 twenty-three | 36 thirty-six | 70 seventy |
| 24 twenty-four | 37 thirty-seven | 80 eighty |
| 25 twenty-five | 38 thirty-eight | 90 ninety |
| 26 twenty-six | 39 thirty-nine | 100 a hundred |

## 2 *Thirteen* or *thirty*? *Fourteen* or *forty*? Listen and write what you hear.

## 3 Say your age, or the age of somebody you know.

*'I'm twenty-three.' 'My mother's fifty.'*

## 4 Practise with numbers.

1. Count: '1, 2, 3, . . .'
2. Count in twos: '2, 4, 6, 8, . . .'
3. Count in fives: '5, 10, 15, . . .'
4. Count backwards: '99, 98, 97, . . .'

## 5 Work in groups or pairs.

1. Say numbers for other students to write.
   *'Fifty-six.'* 56
2. Say numbers for other students to add.
   *'Thirty-eight and seven?' 'Forty-five.'*
3. Say numbers for other students to multiply.
   *'Six sevens?' 'Forty-two.'*

## 6 Spelling. Listen and write the words.
Example: *1. answer*

## 7 Spelling. Work in groups or pairs.

*'How do you spell her?' 'h–e–r.'*
*'Write C–h–i–n–e–s–e.'*

*Chinese*

# Harris & Sanders
## Photographic Supplies
### 13 Old High St, Wembley.

# JOB APPLICATION

Mr/Mrs/Miss/Ms

First name ...................................

Surname ...................................

Age ...................................

Marital status: single ☐
married ☐
divorced ☐
separated ☐
widow(er) ☐

Nationality ...................................

## 8 Fill in the form.

## 9 Copy the form and fill it in with a new identity. Then work with a partner. Ask each other these questions.

1. Mr, Mrs, Miss or Ms?
2. What's your first name?
3. How do you spell it?
4. What's your surname?
5. How do you spell it?
6. How old are you?
7. Where are you from?
8. Are you married?

## 10 Look at the summary on page 135 with your teacher.

13

# People

John  Polly

## A I've got three children

**1** Look at the 'family tree' and complete the sentences. Use your dictionary.

| his her wife husband brother sister |
|---|

1. John is Polly's ............. Polly is John's .............
2. Andrew is Joyce's ............. Joyce is Andrew's .............
3. Polly and John are Joyce's parents. Polly is her mother, and John is ............. father.
4. Andrew and Joyce are John's children. Andrew is his son, and Joyce is ............. daughter.

Andrew  Joyce

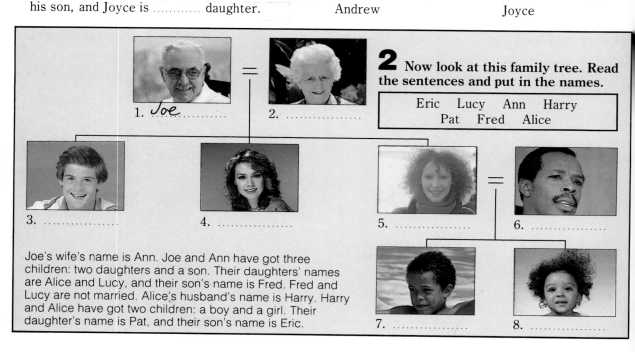

1. *Joe* .............  2. .............

**2** Now look at this family tree. Read the sentences and put in the names.

| Eric  Lucy  Ann  Harry |
| Pat  Fred  Alice |

3. ..............  4. ..............  5. ..............  6. ..............

Joe's wife's name is Ann. Joe and Ann have got three children: two daughters and a son. Their daughters' names are Alice and Lucy, and their son's name is Fred. Fred and Lucy are not married. Alice's husband's name is Harry. Harry and Alice have got two children: a boy and a girl. Their daughter's name is Pat, and their son's name is Eric.

7. ..............  8. ..............

**3** Listening. Look at the family tree in Exercise 1. Listen to the sentences and say *Yes* or *No*.
Make some sentences yourself.

**4** Listening. Look at the family tree in Exercise 2. Listen and answer the questions. Examples:

*'Who is Joe's wife?' 'Ann.'*
*'Who is Eric?' 'Pat's brother.'*

**Then ask some questions yourself.**

**5** Talk about your family. Examples:

*'I've got one child (son/daughter/brother/etc.). His/her name's .............'*
*'How old is he/she?' 'Sixteen.'*

*'I've got two (three etc.) children (sons/daughters/brothers/sisters).'*
*'What are their names?'*

*'I've got no children (brothers or sisters).'*

*'My husband's (wife's/mother's/etc.) name is ............. He/she's thirty-five.'*

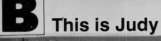

# B This is Judy

| **JUDY** | **SAM** | **ERIC** | **ALICIA** |
|---|---|---|---|
| This is Judy. | This is Sam. | ............. ............. | ............ ............ Eric's girlfriend, ........ |
| She is tall and fair. | He is Judy's boyfriend. | Sam's friend, Eric. | .............................................. |
| She is very pretty. | He is not very ............. | He is ............. | .............................................. |
| . | ............. ............. dark. | and ............. | .............................................. |
| | ............. ............. fairly | He is ........... good- | |
| | good-looking. | looking. | |

**1** Look at the pictures and complete the descriptions.

**2** Describe your mother/father/wife/ husband/boyfriend/girlfriend/brother/sister/ teacher/boss/...

**3** Use your dictionary. Match the words and the pictures.

intelligent   young   slim
fat   strong   old

**4** Work with another student. Make sentences about the two of you. Tell the class.

We're fairly tall.

We're English.

No, you aren't. You're Mexican.

**5** Talk about two other students. Example:

'Mario and Carla are Italian. They're tall and dark.'

**6** Pronunciation revision. Say:

mother   brother   father
Joe's   Harry's   Andrew's   John's
Joyce's   Alice's
who

15

# C An interview

BANK MANAGER: Good morning, Mr Harris.

CUSTOMER: Good morning.

BM: Please sit down.

C: Thank you.

BM: Now, one or two questions...

C: Yes, of course.

BM: How old are you, Mr Harris?

C: Thirty-two.

BM: And you're Canadian, aren't you?

C: Yes, that's right.

BM: Are you married?

C: Yes, I am.

BM: What is your wife's name?

C: Monica.

BM: And your wife's age, Mr Harris?

C: Pardon?

BM: How old is Mrs Harris?

C: Oh, she's thirty.

BM: Thirty. I see. And is she Canadian, too?

C: No, she's British.

BM: British, yes. Have you got any children?

C: Yes, three. Two boys and a girl.

(phone rings)

BM: Excuse me a moment. Hello, Anne. Yes? Yes? Yes, I am. No. Yes. No, I'm sorry, I don't know. No. Yes, all right. Thank you. Goodbye. I'm sorry, Mr Harris.

Now, two girls and a boy, you said?

C: No, two boys and a girl.

BM: Oh, yes, I'm sorry. And what are their names?

C: Alan, Jane and Max.

BM: And their ages?

C: Twelve, ten and six.

BM: I see. Now one more question, Mr Harris. What is your job?

C: I'm a university teacher.

BM: A university teacher. Right. Thank you. Now, you want £50,000 to buy a house.

C: That's right.

BM: And what sort of security...

**1** Listen to the conversation. Then see how much you can remember.

**2** Pronunciation. Practise these expressions.

one or two questions    Yes, of course.
How old are you?    How old is Mrs Harris?
What is your wife's name?    Yes, I am.
two boys and a girl    What are their names?
Twelve, ten and six.

**3** Practise part of the conversation.

**4** Ask and answer. Examples:

Have you got any brothers or sisters?

Yes, I have. I've got two brothers.

No, I haven't.

# D What time is it?

## 1

It's three o'clock.

It's ten past three.

It's a quarter past three.

It's twenty-five past three.

It's half past three.

**What time is it?**

1    2    3    4    5    6    7    8 **9:30**

## 2

It's twenty-five to four.

It's twenty to four.

It's a quarter to four.

It's ten to four.

It's five to four.

**What time is it?**

1    2    3    4    5    6 **2:40**    7 **3:45**    8 **9:55**

## 3 Listening for information. Listen and write down the times you hear.

## 4 Ask another student the time.

*'Excuse me, what time is it?'*

## 5 Grammar revision. Read the text.

Janet and I are both thirty-six. Our children are fourteen, twelve and six. We are tall, and our daughters are both tall for their ages too, but our son is short. We are both fair, but our children are all dark.

**Now read this text. Put in we, our, and, but, are.**

John ............ I ............ from Scotland, ............
............ live in London. ............  ............
both forty. ............ have got three children.
............ daughter, Caroline, is tall ............
fair, ............  ............ two sons, Nicholas
and Thomas, ............ short ............ dark.

## 6 Grammar revision. Put in I, my, you, your, he, his, she, her, we, our, they, their.

1. 'I've got two sisters.' 'How old are ............?' 'Eighteen and fourteen.'
2. Harry and Catherine are tall, and all ............ children are tall, too.
3. Polly is fair, but ............ sister is dark.
4. Hello. My name's Diego. ............'m Spanish.
5. My wife and I are tall, but ............ children are short.
6. 'Is that ............ sister?' 'No, it's my mother.'
7. 'Excuse me, how old are ............?' 'I'm twenty.'
8. John and ............ father are both doctors.
9. Robert isn't very good-looking, but ............'s very intelligent.
10. 'This is Alice. ............'s a photographer.' 'How do ............ do?'
11. ............ husband and I are American, but ............live in England.

## 7 Look at the summary on page 136 with your teacher.

17

# Places

## A Glasgow is an industrial city…

Newcastle, Maryport and Birkby are in the north of England. Newcastle is a large industrial town in the north-east, and Maryport is a small town in the north-west. Birkby is a small village near Maryport.

Dumfries is a small town. It is near Maryport, too, but not in England: it is in the south of Scotland. Crieff, Glasgow and Aberdeen are in Scotland, too. Crieff is in central Scotland, Glasgow is an industrial city on the west coast, and Aberdeen is a large town in the north-east.

Edinburgh is the capital city of Scotland, and a tourist centre. It is on the east coast.

**1** Read the text with help from your teacher.

**2** Pronounce these words.

1. thank thirty north south
2. the their that
3. the doctor the secretary the receptionist the west
4. the artist the electrician the engineer the east

**3** Practise reading the text aloud. Then close your book and remember what you can.

**4** Make more sentences about places on the map. Examples:

'Dundee is a city in the east of Scotland.'
'Arbroath is a town near Dundee.'

**5** Talk about places in other countries. Examples:

'Acapulco is a tourist centre. It is in the south-west of Mexico.'
'Milan is an industrial city in the north of Italy.'

○ VILLAGES
● TOWNS
◉ CITIES

**6** Write about places in your country. Example:

Bilbao is an industrial city in the north of Spain, on the Atlantic coast. Madrid is the capital city of Spain. It is a tourist centre. Barcelona

18

# B Where's that?

## 1 Listen and practise.

A: Oh, that's nice. Where's that?
B: It's Acapulco.
A: That's in Brazil, isn't it?
B: No, it's in Mexico.
A: Oh, yes, of course.

## 2 Draw a picture of a place.

Talk to other students about the picture. Use sentences and expressions from Exercise 1.

## 3 Pronunciation.

| England | India | Japanese |
|---------|-------|----------|
| Brazil | Italy | American |
| Morocco | the west | Italian |
| centre | Russia | Cyprus |

1. Copy the list. Under each word draw a ∿ for stress. Example: England
2. Listen and check your answers.
3. Listen again. Circle ⬭ the vowel where you hear /ə/. Example: England
4. Pronounce the words.

## 4 Prepositions and places. These people are...

at the Kremlin.

on a mountain.

in Paris.

**in, at, or on?**

Venice

the Acropolis

Spain

Mount Everest

Waikiki Beach

the Eiffel Tower

## 5 Listen and practise. Be careful to pronounce *h* correctly.

A: Who's that?
B: It's my husband on the beach in Spain.
A: He's good-looking!
B: Oh, thank you.
A: And the beach is nice, too.
B: Mm.

## 6 Add a person from your family to your picture.

Talk to other students about the picture. Use sentences and expressions from Exercise 5.

# C Where's Stockholm?

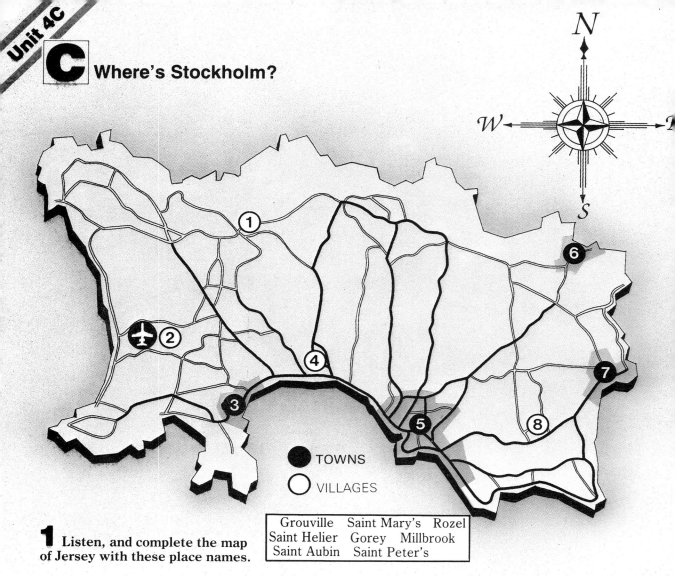

**1** Listen, and complete the map of Jersey with these place names.

● TOWNS
○ VILLAGES

| Grouville | Saint Mary's | Rozel |
| Saint Helier | Gorey | Millbrook |
| Saint Aubin | Saint Peter's | |

**2** Ask and answer questions.

'Where's Cairo?'
'It's in Egypt.'
'Yes, that's right.'

'Where's Canberra?'
'I don't know.'
'It's in Australia.'

'Where's Stockholm?'
'I think it's in Sweden.'
'Yes, that's right.'

'Where's Edinburgh?'
'It's in England.'
'No, it isn't. It's in Scotland.'

Where's Stockholm?

SWEDEN
Stockholm?

**3** Listen to the recording and answer. Examples:

'Montreal's in Canada.' 'That's right.'
'Berlin's in France.' 'No, it isn't.'
'Is Athens in Greece?' 'Yes, it is.'

# D It's an exciting place

Quito, Ecuador

Houston, Texas

## 1 Read the first dialogue, and complete the second one.

A: Where are you from?
B: Texas.
A: Where in Texas?
B: Houston.
A: Oh, the astronauts' city!
B: Yes, it's an exciting place.
   But it's very polluted.

◇

A: Where ........................... ?
B: Ecuador.
A: .......................... Ecuador?
B: ............ .
A: ............................... nice?
B: Yes, ............ a pretty city,
   ............ very exciting, too.

## 2 With another student, ask and answer questions about your village/town/city. Here are some words to help you:

| quiet | pretty | noisy |
| nice | polluted | exciting |

## 3 Tell the class (or another student) about your partner's village/town/city. Example:

'Marianne is from Vézelay, near Avallon, in France. It's a small village, and it's very pretty. It's quiet, and it's not very exciting.'

## 4 In pairs: choose a town or city. Write two sentences about it. Read them to the other students. Example:

'It is a city on the east coast of the United States. It is polluted and noisy, but it is exciting.'
'Is it Boston?' 'No, it isn't.'
'Is it New York?' 'Yes, it is.'

## 5 Say the numbers after your teacher.

| 101 | a hundred and one |
| 132 | a hundred and thirty-two |
| 300 | three hundred |
| 354 | three hundred and fifty-four |
| 1,000 | a thousand (one thousand) |
| 1,400 | one thousand four hundred |
| 1,000,000 | a million (one million) |

## 6 Ask and answer.

What's the population of Tokyo?

I don't know.

About 9 million, I think.

About 2 million.

What's the population of Toronto?

Six hundred and thirty-three thousand, three hundred and eighteen.

| Cairo | 8,500,000 |
| London | 7,028,200 |
| Mexico | 8,591,750 |
| Rio de Janeiro | 5,157,000 |
| Singapore | 2,147,400 |
| Lagos | 1,060,848 |
| Munich | 1,314,865 |
| Toronto | 633,318 |

## 7 Look at the summary on page 137 with your teacher.

# Home

## A  A house

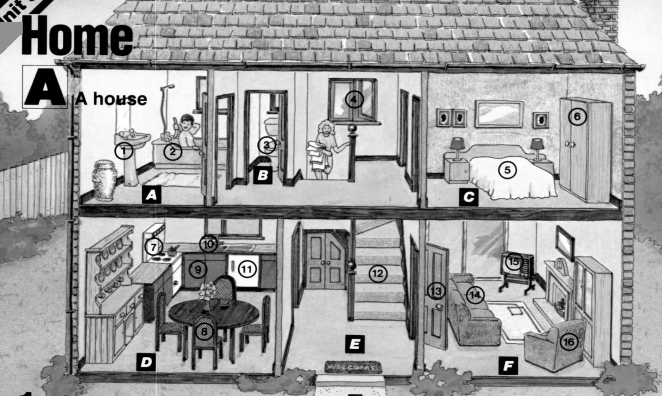

**1** Look at the picture, and put the words with the right letters. Use your dictionary or work with other students. Example:

*A. bathroom*

| | | | |
|---|---|---|---|
| bedroom | kitchen | bathroom | living room |
| | hall | toilet | |

**2** Now put these words with the right numbers.

chair   bed   toilet   door   window   stairs
cooker   sofa   fridge   armchair
television (TV)   cupboard   wardrobe   sink
washbasin   bath

**3** The teacher's home.
Listen to the description.

**4** Complete the sentences, and make some more sentences about the house in the picture.

1. There are ............ bedrooms in the house.
2. There is (There's) an armchair ............ the living room.
3. ............ is not a garage.
4. There ............ ............ bathroom.
5. There ............ two toilets.
6. ............ ............ fridge in the kitchen.

**5** Work in pairs.

1. Both students copy the plan.
2. One student furnishes his or her rooms.
3. The other asks questions beginning
   *Is there a...?* or *Are there any...?*
4. He or she listens to the answers and tries to put the right furniture etc. into the rooms.

**Examples:**

'*Is there a fridge in the kitchen?*'
   '*Yes, there is.*' (Or '*No, there isn't.*')

'*Are there any chairs in the bathroom?*'
   '*No, there aren't.*' (Or '*Yes, there are two.*')

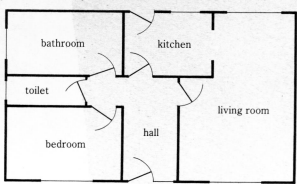

**6** Draw a plan of your house (or your 'dream house') and write five sentences about it.

22

# B Where do you live?

ninth (9th) floor
eighth (8th) floor
seventh (7th) floor
sixth (6th) floor
fifth (5th) floor
fourth (4th) floor
third (3rd) floor
second (2nd) floor
first (1st) floor
ground floor

## 1 Look at the pictures. Put the words in the right places.

The Prime Minister lives at 10 Downing Street.
My sister works in Edinburgh.
'Where do you live, Mary?' 'In Aston Street.'
'What's your address?' '39 Morrison Avenue.'
We live in a small flat on the fourth floor.

Mrs L. Williams
17 Harcourt Road
Coventry
West Midlands CY2 4BJ

## 2 At, in or on?

1. I live ............ 37 Valley Road.
2. 'Where do you work?' '............ New York.'
3. My office is ............ the fourteenth floor.
4. Jake lives ............ a big old house ............ Washington.
5. 'Where do you live?' '............ 116 New Street.'

## 3 Ask the addresses of some other students and write them down.

'Excuse me. What's your address?'
'16 Grange Road. Where do you live?'
'At 17 Queen's Drive.'

## 4
a) What floor do you live/work on?
  **Examples:** '*I live on the third floor.*'
  '*I work on the seventh floor.*'
b) Where are you now?
  **Example:** '*We're on the first floor.*'
c) What floor does your father/mother/brother/boss etc. work/live on?
  **Example:** '*My mother lives on the fourth floor.*'

## 5 Listening for information. Listen to the conversations, and write the correct letters after the names. (There are only three phone numbers.)

| NAME | LIVES | PHONE NUMBER |
|---|---|---|
| John | | X |
| Peter Matthews | | |
| Alice's mother | | |
| Mr Billows | | |
| Mrs Webber | G | |
| Mrs Simon | | |

A  at 16 Norris Road, Bedford.
B  in a small flat in North London.
C  in Birmingham.
D  at 116 Market Street.
E  in New York.
F  on the fourth floor.
G  at 60 Hamilton Road, Gloucester.

V  314 6928
W  41632
X  314 6829
Y  41785
Z  41758

# C What's your phone number?

| | | | |
|---|---|---|---|
| A | 472 1067 | F | 444 6704 |
| B | 668 6154 | G | 238 1176 |
| C | 831 7541 | H | 781 8254 |
| D | 374 6522 | I | 904 0799 |
| E | 551 0723 | J | 235 1600 |

**2** Listen again. Answer '*Yes, hello*' or
'*No, sorry, wrong number.*'

**3** What's your phone number? Ask the
phone numbers of the students sitting near
you. Example:

'*Excuse me. What's your phone number?*'
'*Three one four double two oh seven.*'
'*Three one four double two oh seven?*'
'*Yes, that's right.*'
'*Thanks.*'
'*What's your phone number?*' etc.

**4** Listen to the two conversations and study them. Then
make similar conversations and practise them with a partner.

MARIA: Hello. Oxford 49382.
ALICE: Hello. Could I speak to Maria,
please?
MARIA: Speaking. Who's that?
ALICE: This is Alice.
MARIA: Oh, hello, Alice. How are you?
ALICE: Fine, thanks. Listen, Maria, I...

JOE: Hello.
BILL: Hello. Could I speak to Sally,
please?
JOE: One moment, please...I'm
sorry. She's not here. Can I take
a message?
BILL: Pardon?
JOE: Can I take a message?
BILL: Yes. Could you tell her that Bill
called?
JOE: Yes, of course.
BILL: Thanks very much. Goodbye.
JOE: You're welcome. Goodbye.

# D  More than one

| SINGULAR | PLURAL /z/ |
|---|---|
| room | rooms |
| table | tables |
| chair | chairs |
| boy | boys |
| family | families |
| secretary | secretaries |

| SINGULAR | PLURAL /s/ |
|---|---|
| bank | banks |
| flat | flats |
| artist | artists |
| parent | parents |
| bath | baths |
| shop | shops |

| SINGULAR | PLURAL /ɪz/ |
|---|---|
| address | addresses |
| watch | watches |
| dish | dishes |
| place | places |
| village | villages |
| fridge | fridges |

| SINGULAR | PLURAL (irregular) |
|---|---|
| man | men |
| woman (/'wʊmən/) | women (/'wɪmɪn/) |
| child (/tʃaɪld/) | children (/'tʃɪldrən/) |
| person | people |
| wife | wives |
| house (/haʊs/) | houses (/'haʊzɪz/) |

**1** **Study the pronunciation of the plural nouns. Can you say these words?**

rooms  tables  flats  watches  chairs
places  afternoons  toilets  tourists
windows  centres  garages  beds  cities
cookers  messages  sofas  sisters

**2** **Write the plurals of these words.**

field  book  bus  bully  day  trip
try  ash  tree  toy  diary  tiger
sock  match  boss

**3** **Make the following expressions plural.**

a good-looking artist

*good-looking artists*

a French student

*French students*

her teacher

*her teachers*

a tall man
a nice person
our friend
a shop assistant
a nice accountant
my aunt
an intelligent girl
a Spanish village
their secretary
a fair woman
his child
a small job
a large city
a dark room

**4** **Read the postcard. Work with a partner and write a similar holiday postcard to a friend.**

Dear Mary,
Well, here we are at Première
Miami Beach. At last!
Our hotel is very nice and
the food's good. We're on
the 14th floor! Our room
is small, but it's clean
and quiet. There are
some nice people from
Manchester in the
next room.
    love, Carol and Jim

Mrs Mary Anderson
14, Windrush Road
Cartmel
Cumbria
GREAT BRITAIN

**5** Look at the summary on page 138 with your teacher.

# Habits

## A What do you like?

Jackson Pollock: Yellow Island

Greek bronze

Vermeer: Young Girl

Mexican mask

**1** Look at the pictures and sculpture. Which one do you like? Examples:

*'I like the Greek bronze very much.'*
*'I quite like the mask.'*
*'I neither like nor dislike the mask.'*
*'I don't like the Vermeer picture much.'*
*'I hate the Pollock picture. I don't like it at all.'*
*'I like the Greek bronze best.'*

**2** Listen to the music and sounds and say whether you like them or not.

I like it very much.

I don't like it at all.

**3** Put in *like, likes, it* or *them.*

1. I don't ............ cats, but my brother ............ them very much.
2. 'Do you ............ dogs?' 'Yes, I love ............'
3. George ............ Mary, but Mary doesn't like him.
4. Mary ............ dancing and travelling.
5. 'Do you ............ whisky?' 'No, I don't like ............ at all.'
6. I don't dislike opera, but I don't really ............ ............
7. 'Your husband ............ cooking, doesn't he?' 'Yes, he does.'
8. My wife hates big dogs, but I love ............
9. My wife and I ............ the sea, but our children don't – they ............ climbing mountains.
10. 'Do you ............ Anne?' 'Yes, I ............ her very much.'

**4** Do you like these? Ask other students about one of them.

big dogs  maths  whisky  mountains  the sea  cats  shopping
watching TV  cooking  dancing  writing letters  travelling

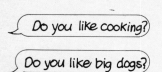

Do you like cooking?

Do you like big dogs?

Yes, I do.

No, I don't.

I love it / them.

I hate it / them.

It depends.

**5** Report to the class. Examples:

*'Seven students like cats.'*
*'Five people like big dogs.'*
*'Only two people like shopping.'*
*'Only one person like<u>s</u> maths.'*
*'Jean-Claude like<u>s</u> whisky very much.'*
*'Nobody like<u>s</u> cooking.'*
*'Everybody like<u>s</u> the sea.'*

# B Work

## 1 Put the words into the text.

Stan Dixon is a shop assistant. He sells men's clothes in a small shop. It is a tiring job.
Stan ............ at seven o'clock. After .........., he ............ to work by ............ He .......... work at a quarter past nine; the shop .......... at half past. Stan ............ lunch at twelve, and then ............ from 12.45 until .45.
On Saturdays, Stan ............ work at one o'clock. On Sundays he ............ cycling or .......... tennis.
Stan does not ............ his job much.

| | | | |
|---|---|---|---|
| has | like | breakfast | goes |
| works | bus | gets up | opens |
| stops | plays | starts | goes |

## 2 Do it yourself. Ask the teacher questions, and write the text about Karen Miller.

Karen Miller is a mechanic. She repairs cars in a garage. . . .

| |
|---|
| What time does she get up? |
| Does she have breakfast? |
| How \| go to work? |
| What time \| start work? |
| What time \| stop work? |
| What time \| have lunch? |
| \| work on Saturdays? |
| What \| do at the weekend? |
| \| like her job? |

## 3 Stan Dixon and Karen Miller both have lunch at twelve. Find out two more things that they both do.

## 4 Put in the correct verb forms.

1. Stan ............ breakfast at half past seven. (have/has)
2. Karen does not ............ breakfast. (have/has)
3. How does Karen ............ to work? (go/goes)
4. Stan ............ to work by bus. (go/goes)
5. My father ............ in Cardiff. (work/works)
6. He does not ............ travelling. (like/likes)
7. He ............ at six o'clock every day. (get up/gets up)
8. He does not ............ on Saturdays. (work/works)
9. My parents ............ in a big flat. (live/lives)
10. What does your father ............? (do/does)

## 5 Learn the days of the week.

### MARCH

| | | | | | |
|---|---|---|---|---|---|
| Monday | | 5 | 12 | 19 | 26 |
| Tuesday | | 6 | 13 | 20 | 27 |
| Wednesday | | 7 | 14 | 21 | 28 |
| Thursday | 1 | 8 | 15 | 22 | 29 |
| Friday | 2 | 9 | 16 | 23 | 30 |
| Saturday | 3 | 10 | 17 | 24 | 31 |
| Sunday | 4 | 11 | 18 | 25 | |

# C What newspaper do you read?

| | |
|---|---|
| NEWSPAPER | I read ........................................................ . |
| BOOKS | I read ........................................................ . |
| | I don't read ................................................. . |
| FOOD | I like ........................................................ . |
| | I don't like ................................................. . |
| DRINK | I like ........................................................ . |
| | I don't like ................................................. . |
| SPORT | I play ........................................................ . |
| | I don't play ................................................. . |
| | I watch ........................................................ . |
| MUSIC | I like ........................................................ . |
| | I don't like ................................................. . |
| | I play ........................................................ . |
| INTERESTS | I'm interested in ........................................... . |
| | ................................................................ . |
| LANGUAGES | I speak ........................................................ . |
| | I don't speak ............................................... . |
| HOLIDAYS | I often go (to) ............................. on holiday. |
| ACTIVITIES | I like ..................................................... ing. |
| | I like ..................................................... ing. |
| | I don't like ............................................. ing. |

**1** Fill in the table. The teacher will help you.

**2** Listen to the recording and answer the questions. Examples:

*'Are you married?' 'Yes, I am.' / 'No, I'm not.'*
*'Do you like music?' 'Yes, I do.' / 'No, I don't.'*
*'What sort of music do you like?' 'Rock.'*

**3** Interview the teacher. Ask him or her questions about his or her day, interests etc. Possible questions:

What time do you get up?
Do you have breakfast?
How do you travel to work?
What time do you start work?
　　　　　　　　have lunch?
　　　　　　　　stop work?
What do you do in the evenings?
　　　　　　　　at the weekend?
What newspaper do you read?
Do you like reading?
What sort of books do you like?
Do you like science fiction?
Do you like fish?
What sort of food do you like?
Do you like beer?
Do you play tennis?
Do you like skiing?
Do you watch football?
Do you like music?
Do you play an instrument?
Are you interested in politics?
What languages do you speak?
Where do you go on holiday?

**4** Interview another student. Spend five minutes with him or her, and try to find:

1. Five negative facts (for example, *'He doesn't play tennis.'*).
2. Five things that you both have in common (for example, *'We both like the sea.'*).

**5** Write about the student you interviewed.

# D What does Lorna drink?

**1** Listening for information. Listen to the recording and complete the table. Put a ✓ for the things each person drinks. Part of Lorna's table is done for you.

|       | Coffee | Wine | Gin | Beer | Tea |
|-------|--------|------|-----|------|-----|
| Lorna | ✓      | ✓    |     |      |     |
| Katy  |        |      |     |      |     |
| Pat   |        |      |     |      |     |
| Ruth  |        |      |     |      |     |

**2** Pronunciation. Where are the stresses?

1. What does she do? Where does she work? How does she go to work?
2. Where do you live? What time do you stop work? Do you work on Saturdays?
3. Yes, I do. No, I don't. Yes, he does. No, he doesn't.

**3** Listening to fast speech. How many words are there? What are they? Contractions like *what's* count as two words.

'No thanks – I don't drink.'

**4** Grammar revision.

**A. Put in *do*, *don't*, *does* or *doesn't*.**
1. '............ you like fish?' 'Yes, I ............'
2. Where ............ Sally live?
3. I'm sorry, I ............ know.
4. '............ your mother work?' 'No, she ............'
5. What newspaper ............ you read?
6. What newspaper ............ your father read?

**B. Make questions.**
1. you | tired? *Are you tired?*
2. Lucy | like beer? *Does Lucy like beer?*
3. Where | your father | work?
4. they | work on Saturdays?
5. Alex and Jimmie | like skiing?
6. she | German?
7. What time | you | stop work?
8. your sister | pretty?

**5** Look at the summary on page 139 with your teacher.

29

# Food and drink

### A  How many calories?

7. a litre of ☐  ☐ ca

5. half a litre of ☐
☐ calories

3. 100ml of ☐
☐ calories

4. an ☐
☐ calories

2. 150g of ☐
☐ calories

6. a ☐
☐ calories

1. 100ml of ☐
☐ calories

8. 50g of ☐
☐ calories

9. an ☐
☐ calories

10. 750g of ☐  ☐ calories

11. a ☐
☐ calories

12. a ☐
☐ calories

**1** What are the names of the things in the picture? Try to put the words in the right places.

tomato   egg   water   rump steak   potato
cheese   bread   orange   whisky   milk
wine   banana

**2** How many calories? Try to put the right numbers with the pictures.

| 0 | 7 | 40 | 70 | 80 | 90 |
|---|---|----|----|----|----|
| 115 | 175 | 200 | 320 | 636 | 1275 |

**3** Listen to the recording of people guessing how many calories there are.

**4** Can you complete the lists?

C an egg, a tomato, ...
U wine, cheese, ...

**5** C or U?

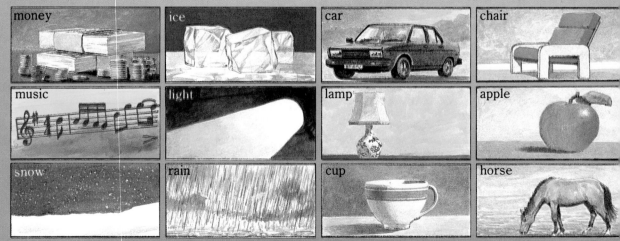

money

ice

car

chair

music

light

lamp

apple

snow

rain

cup

horse

**6** Pronunciation. Try to say these words with the right stress.

tomato   potato   orange   whisky   banana   calorie   family   bathroom   television
wardrobe   furniture   intelligent   boyfriend   eleven   thirty   thirteen

# B It's terrible

- It's terrible.
- The prices
- Oh, dear.
- Do you know potatoes are eighty pence a kilo?
- Eighty pence a kilo? In our supermarket they're eighty-five.
- It's terrible.
- Oh, dear.
- Everything's so expensive.
- Do you know tomatoes are £1.20 a kilo?
- £1.20? In our supermarket they're £1.30.
- No!!!
- Yes!
- It's terrible.
- Milk's seventy-five pence a litre.
- Half a kilo of rump steak is £7.50.
- An orange costs 20p. One orange!
- And cheese!
- I know!
- Do you know, yesterday I was in Patterson's
- Were you?
- Yes, and cheese was £6.30 a kilo.
- £6.30?
- Yes, and bananas were £2.25.
- It's terrible.

**1** Listen to the conversation (books closed) and answer the teacher's questions.

**2** Say these words and expressions.

It's **terrible**
**eigh**ty **pence** a **ki**lo
Potatoes are **eigh**ty **pence** a **ki**lo.
In our supermarket
they're eighty-five.
expensive
Everything's so expensive.
tomatoes are **one pound twen**ty
**one pound twen**ty a **ki**lo
**half** a **ki**lo
an orange
I was in Patterson's
Do you know?
bananas were **two pounds twen**ty-**five**

**3** Practise the conversation.

**4** Make short conversations in groups of four or five.

**5** Put in *a/an* where necessary.

1. ...A... kilo of rump steak is very expensive.
2. There are 424 calories in 100g of ........... cheese.
3. ........... potatoes are not very expensive.
4. ........... orange is 20p.
5. There are 7 calories in ........... tomato.
6. There are no calories in ........... water.
7. 'How much are ........... bananas?' '£2.25 a kilo.'
8. ........... wine is expensive in Britain.

**6** Put in *is, are, was* or *were*.

1. Yesterday I ........... in London.
2. Steak ........... very expensive.
3. Yesterday my mother and father ........... in Manchester.
4. Oranges ........... £1.40 a kilo.
5. In 1960, oranges ........... 20p a kilo and a bottle of wine ........... 60p.

# C  Have you got a good memory?

**1** Find out the names of the animals etc. (Ask your teacher.)

**2** Talk about the picture. Examples:

'There's some water in the big field.'
'There are some pigs in the small field.'
'There are some sheep on the mountain.'

**3** Have you got a good memory? Close your book, listen and answer the questions. Examples:

'Is there any grass on the mountain?'
'Yes, there is.'

'Are there any chickens in the big field?'
'No, there aren't.'

'I don't remember.'

**4** Write five questions about the picture. Close your book. Ask another student your questions, and answer his or her questions.

**5** Listen to the questions. Answer:

'Yes, there is.'        'No, there isn't.'
'Yes, there's one.'     'No, there aren't.'
'Yes, there are.'

**6** Make sentences.

There isn't
There aren't / any / ............. /
in my house.
in my flat.
in this room.
in my pocket.
etc.

| YES | ? | NO |
|---|---|---|
| There is some water. | Is there any water? | There isn't any water. |
| There are some cows. | Are there any cows? | There aren't any cows. |

# D Not enough money

**1** Quiz. Put *how much* or *how many*; answer the questions. Make some questions yourself.

1. ............ ............ states are there in the USA – 36, 49, 50 or 60?
2. ............ ............ wine is there in a normal bottle – 75cl, 85cl or 95cl?
3. ............ ............ Coca Cola is drunk in the world in one day – one million bottles, 11 million bottles or 110 million bottles?

4. ............ ............ planets (Mercury, Venus etc.) are there – 7, 9, 11 or 13?
5. ............ ............ of a person is water – 40%, 60% or 90%?
6. ............ ............ keys are there on a piano – 70, 82 or 88?
7. ............ ............ air is there in our lungs – half a litre, one and a half litres or two and a half litres?
8. ............ ............ Beatles were there – 3, 4 or 5?

**2** Listen to the recording of people trying to do the quiz.

**3** Listen, and choose the right words for each situation.
Example: 1. *'not many people'*

not much
not many
a lot of

people   cats   cigarettes
students   food   money
time   water   girlfriends

**4** Talk about the classroom. Begin:

*'There isn't much ...'*
*'There aren't many ...'*
*'There is/are a lot of ...'*

**5** Look at the pictures and choose the right words.

not enough
too much
too many

people   toothpaste
hair   perfume   light   shaving cream   money
cars   toilets   children   chips   hair   numbers

**6** Talk about yourself.

*'I've got enough/too much/too many ...'*
*'I haven't got enough ...'*

**7** Look at the summary on page 140 with your teacher.

# Where?

## A  Where's the nearest post office?

**1** Put the words with the correct pictures.

> phone box   supermarket   bank   post office
> police station   car park   bus stop   station

**2** Listen and practise these dialogues.

A: Excuse me. Where's the nearest post office,
   please?
B: It's over there on the | right ⟩ / ⟨ left. |
A: Oh, thank you very much.
B: Not at all.

—◇—

A: Excuse me. Where's the nearest bank, please?
B: I'm sorry, I don't know.
A: Thank you anyway.

**3** Complete these dialogues and
practise them.

A: ............  .............  ............ the manager's
   office, ............?
B: ............  ............  ............ by the
   reception desk.
A: ............  .............

—◇—

A: ............  .............  ............  ............ the
   toilets, ............?
B: Upstairs ............ the first floor, first
   door ............  ............ left.
A: ............  ............  ............ much.

**4** Make up similar conversations
and practise them.

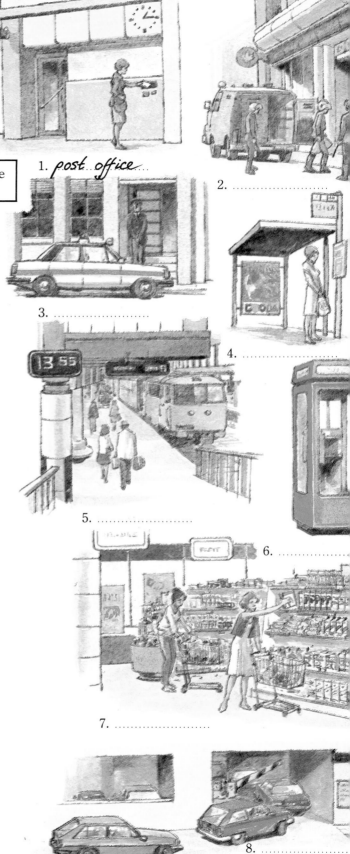

1. *post office*

2. ........................

3. ........................

4. ........................

5. ........................

6. ........................

7. ........................

8. ........................

# B First on the right, second on the left

**1** Put in the missing words, separate the two conversations, and put the sentences in the right order.

'Yes. It's ............................ the car park. Go ............................
for about three hundred ............................,'
'Excuse me. ............................ the nearest car park,
............................?'
'Thank you very much.'
'............................ on the right, then second .............................
It's next to the post office.'
'............................ is it?'
'............................,'
'............................. Is there a ............................ near here?'
'Thanks very much.'
'About five hundred yards.'

> first    please    not at all    opposite    where's
> on the left    how far    straight on    excuse me
> yards    swimming pool

**2** Look at the map. Then work with another student and test his or her memory.

'*Where's the police station?' 'Opposite the railway station.'*
'*Where's the car park?' 'I don't remember.'*

**3** Listen and follow the directions on the map. Then say where you are.

**4** Give directions to other students. Example:

'*You are at A. Take the first left, second right, first right, second right, and go straight on for about three hundred metres. Where are you?'*

**5** Copy the map. Then put in *either* the places in list A *or* the places in list B.

A. a supermarket
   a swimming pool
   a bookshop
   a phone box
   a cheap restaurant
   a cheap hotel

B. a church
   a good restaurant
   a good hotel
   a chemist's
   a public toilet

**Work in pairs. Ask and give directions (you are at A on the map). Example:**

'*Excuse me. Is there a bookshop near here, please?'*
'*Yes. First left, second right, in Station Road.'*
'*Thank you.'*

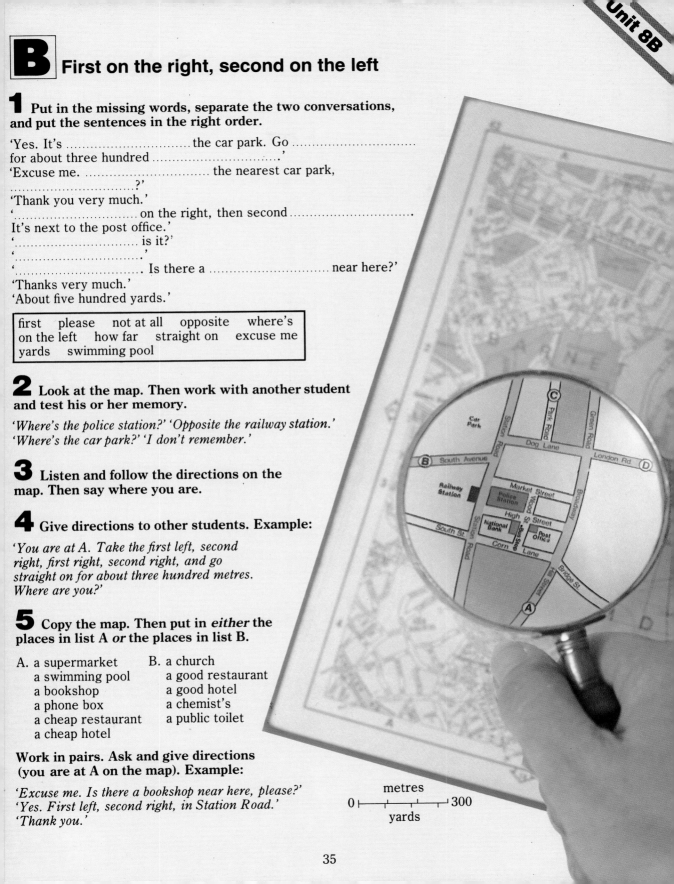

metres
0 ⊢——⊢——⊢——⊣ 300
yards

35

# C Where are they?

## 1 Listen to the conversation. Where is Simon's house?

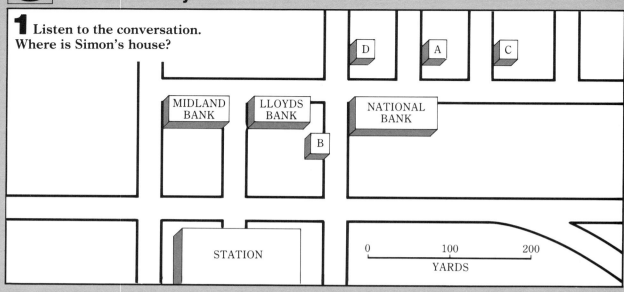

## 2 Listen to the conversation. Which flat is Sally's?

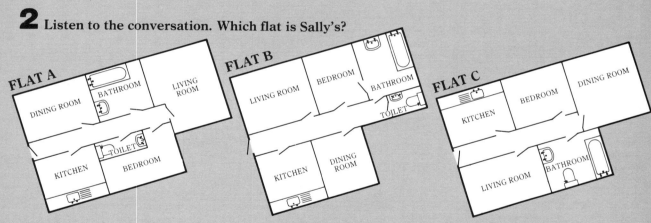

## 3 Listen to the conversations. Where are the people?

| Nelly | |
| --- | --- |
| Mrs Jackson | |
| Jane | |
| Alice | E |
| John | |

A  at the station
B  at the supermarket
C  at the bank
D  at home
E  we don't know
F  at the swimming pool

## 4 Listen to the recording of somebody asking the way. Do all the people give the same answer?

## 5 Pronunciation. Mark the stresses in these sentences and practise saying them.

How do you do?
Where are you from?
Polly and John are Joyce's parents.
My mother and I are both tall.
Two boys and a girl.
What are their names?
There are two bedrooms in my flat.
What's your address?
I live at twenty-two New Street.
A litre of water.
A kilo of potatoes.
Everything's so expensive.
My birthday is on March the twenty-first.
First on the right, second on the left.

# D  I'm hungry

1. She is ............
2. He is ............
3. She is ............
4. He is ............
5. She is ............
6. He is ............
7. She is ............
8. He is ............
9. She is ............
10. He is ............

**1** Put the adjectives with the right pictures.

> hungry   tired   wet   happy   cold   dirty
> bored   unhappy   thirsty   hot

**2** Say how you feel now.

'I'm hungry.' 'I'm thirsty.' 'I'm fine.'

**3** Mime one of the adjectives for the class.

You're unhappy.

**4** You're in one of these places. Do a mime; the class will say where you are.

> at a swimming pool   at a disco   at a cinema
> at a pub   at a restaurant   in bed
> in the bathroom   at a car park   at the doctor's
> at the dentist's   at a supermarket   at home
> at school   at a bus stop

**5** Have you got a good memory? Look at the sentences for two minutes. Then close your books and answer the teacher's questions.

When Fred's hungry he goes to a restaurant.
When Lucy's hungry she has bread and cheese.
When Fred's thirsty he goes to a pub.
When Lucy's thirsty she has a drink of water.
When Fred's bored he goes to the cinema.
When Lucy's bored she watches TV.
When Fred's hot he goes to the swimming pool.
When Lucy's hot she has a drink of water.
When Fred's dirty he has a bath.
When Lucy's dirty she has a wash.
When Fred's happy he sings.
When Lucy's happy she dances.
When Fred's unhappy he goes to bed.
When Lucy's unhappy she has a bath.

**6** Look at the summary on page 141 with your teacher.

# The World

## A How people live

**1** Separate the two mixed-up texts. Work in groups. Use dictionaries, but not too much.

AUSTRALIAN ABORIGINES
AMAZON INDIANS

The Karadjere people live in the desert of Western
  Australia,
These people live in the Amazon Basin, in Brazil,
where the climate is very hot.
where the climate is hot and wet:
and the rest of the year is dry.
It rains from January to March,
it rains for nine to ten months of the year.

They travel by canoe.
They do not live in one place,
They live in villages;
but travel around on foot.
They sleep in shelters made of dry tree branches.
and the roofs are made of palm leaves.
their houses are made of wood,
Several families live in each house.

Their food is fruit, nuts and kangaroo meat,
They eat fruit and vegetables, fish, and meat
  from animals and birds
and they eat fish in the wet season;
(for example monkeys, wild pigs, parrots).
they also make bread from grass seeds.
The Karadjere like music, dancing and telling
  stories.
They like music, dancing and telling stories.
Water is often difficult to find.
They do not wear many clothes.
They do not wear many clothes.

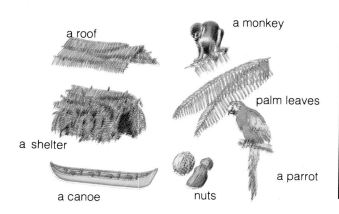

a roof

a monkey

a shelter

palm leaves

a canoe

nuts

a parrot

**2** What do you know about the Eskimos' traditional way of life? Write what you know in a short text.

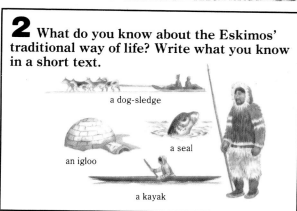

a dog-sledge

an igloo

a seal

a kayak

**3** How do you think most Eskimos live today?

38

# B What do parrots eat?

## 1 Put these words with the correct pictures.

gorilla   camel   parrot   snake   polar bear
tiger   penguin   elephant

## 2 Make true or false sentences about where animals live.
Examples:

Penguins live in the Arctic.

I know.   Do they?   Are you sure?   No, they don't. They live in the Antarctic.

## 3 How sure are you? Make sentences about what animals eat. Use *I know (that)*; *I'm sure (that)*; *certainly*; *I think (that)*; *perhaps*; *I don't think (that)*. Examples:

'*Penguins certainly eat fish. I think (that) parrots eat nuts. Perhaps snakes eat grass. I don't think (that) cats eat insects.*'

meat   fish   grass   nuts   insects   leaves   fruit

## 4 Pronunciation.

gorilla   parrot   polar   tiger   elephant   Australia
Brazil   Amazon   America   Germany   Italy   China
Japan   Canada

1. **Underline the stressed syllable in each word.**
   Example: _gorilla_
2. **Listen and check your answers.**
3. **Listen again. Circle the vowel (*a, e, i, o* or *u*)
   where you hear /ə/. Example:** g(o)rilla
4. **Pronounce the words.**

## 5 Pronunciation. Say these words.

eat   meat   leaves   sleep   these   people
seeds   peanuts

it   village   fish   live   in   pig   this
difficult   women   think

# CD The weather

## THE WEATHER IN EAST TEXAS

In East Texas, near the Gulf of Mexico, the climate is hot and often very humid. Temperatures in summer are between 30° and 40°C; 25°C is a normal winter temperature. It is sometimes cold, but only for two or three days at a time; it snows perhaps once every twenty years. It quite often rains heavily for two or three days or more, but most of the time it is sunny with bright blue skies. Occasionally there are droughts – periods when there is no rain for a long time. It is not usually very windy, but there are hurricanes every few years.

**1** Read the text about the weather in East Texas. Use a dictionary or get your teacher to help you.

**2** Now read the text about the weather in Britain. Fill in the blanks with these words and expressions.

| | | |
|---|---|---|
| skies | but | fairly |
| temperature | | short |
| rains | know | changeable |
| people | | winters |
| sometimes | long | at a time |
| often | weather | does |

## THE WEATHER IN BRITAIN

In Britain, the ............ is very ............: it ............ a lot, but the sun often shines too. ............ can be ............ cold, with an average ............ of 5°C in the south; there is often snow.

　　Summers can be cool or warm, but the temperature ............ not usually go above 30°C. It is ............ cloudy, and there are ............ grey ............ for days or weeks ............

Days are ............ in summer and ............ in winter. There is sometimes fog, ............ not so often as foreigners think. British ............ never ............ what tomorrow's weather will be like.

Reports for the 24 hours to 6 pm on August 3

| | Sun-shine hrs. | Rain in | Max. Temp. C | F | Weather (day) |
|---|---|---|---|---|---|
| London | 11.2 | — | 25 | 77 | Sunny |
| Birmingham | 10.5 | — | 25 | 77 | Sunny |
| Bristol | 10.2 | — | 26 | 79 | Sunny |
| Cardiff | 9.8 | — | 24 | 75 | Sunny |
| Anglesey | 3.2 | — | 20 | 68 | Rain pm |
| Blackpool | 5.8 | — | 21 | 70 | Bright |
| Manchester | 8.3 | — | 24 | 75 | Sunny |
| ......ham | 10.9 | .03 | 26 | 79 | Sunny |
| | | | 21 | 70 | Drizzle p |

**3** How often? Put these expressions on the line between NEVER and ALL THE TIME.

| not very often   quite often   sometimes |
| occasionally   often   once every twenty years |
| very often |

NEVER                          *quite often*                      ALL THE TIME

0    1    2    3    4    5    6    7    8    9    10

**4** Fill in the table with information from the two texts. Use the following words and expressions: *very often, often, quite often, sometimes, occasionally, once every ... years, never, don't know.*

| WEATHER | | GB | TEXAS |
|---|---|---|---|
| sun | ☼ | | |
| rain | | | |
| snow | | | |
| fog | | *sometimes* | |
| hurricanes | | | |
| droughts | $H_2O$ | *don't know* | |
| temperatures above 30°C | 35°c | | |

**5** Say some things about the weather in your country. Use the words *often, sometimes, occasionally, never* in some of your sentences.

**6** Look at these three ways of talking about the weather.

| WITH A VERB | WITH A NOUN | WITH AN ADJECTIVE |
|---|---|---|
| It often **rains**. | There is often **rain**. | It is often **rainy** (or **wet**). |

Put these words into the correct columns: *sunny, sun, hot, snows, snow, wind, windy, cold, cool, cloud, cloudy, warm, foggy, fog.*

**7** Listening for information. Copy the table. Listen to the recording and circle the expressions which you hear.

| TODAY: | (another good day)   not a good day |
| | sunshine   rain   drought |
| TOMORROW: | it'll cloud over   tomorrow evening   showers |
| | today   warm   temperatures   36–37 maximum |
| SUNDAY: | rather cloudy   a few showers |
| | not much cooler |
| MONDAY: | sun   very hot   normal temperatures |

**8** What will the weather be like tomorrow? Say what you think. Write your forecast and check tomorrow. Examples:

'It will rain.'
'It will be cloudy.'
'There will be snow.'

**9** Look at the summary on page 142 with your teacher.

'I'm afraid it's the weather.'

41

# Appearances

## A  Sheila has got long dark hair

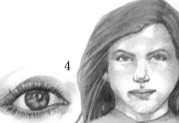

1

2

3

4

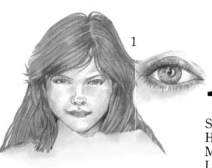

**1** Put the right names with the pictures.

Sheila has got long dark hair and brown eyes.
Helen has got long red hair and green eyes.
Mary has got long fair hair and green eyes.
Lucy has got short grey hair and blue eyes.

**2** Ask the teacher questions.

What's this?

It's your mouth.

What are these?

Ears.

**3** Test other students. Do they know these words?

hair    eyes    nose    ears    mouth    face
arm    hand    foot    leg

TOUCH YOUR RIGHT EYE.

TOUCH YOUR LEFT EAR.

**4** Talk about yourself and other people. Examples:

'I've got small hands. My mother has got pretty hair.'

**5** Write three sentences with *and*, and three with *but*. Examples:

*I've got blue eyes, and my mother has, too. I've got straight hair, but my brother's got curly hair.*

**6** Listening for information. Listen to the recording and fill in the table.

| | height | hair colour | face | eyes | good-looking? |
|---|---|---|---|---|---|
| Steve's wife | 5ft 8 | | | | don't know |
| Lorna's mum | | | pale | | |
| Ruth's friend | | | | | |
| Katy's son | | | | | |
| Sue's husband | | | | | |

# B  A red sweater and blue jeans

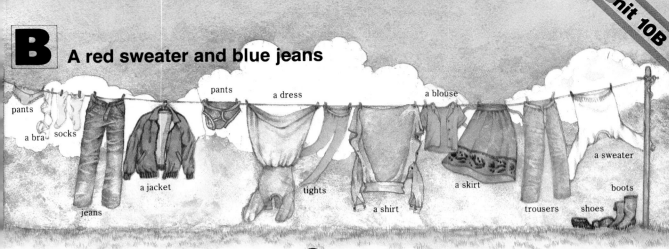

pants
a bra  socks
a jacket
jeans
pants  a dress
tights
a shirt
a blouse
a skirt
trousers  shoes
a sweater
boots

**1** Can you find something red in the classroom? Something blue? Something orange? . . .

**2** Look at the pictures.
Pat is wearing a white sweater and a red and black skirt.

**Make some more sentences about Pat, Keith, Annie and Robert.**
'Keith is wearing. . .'

Pat

Keith

Robert  Annie

**3** Look at another student. Then close your eyes and describe him/her. Example:

'Carlos is wearing blue jeans and a black shirt. I can't remember the colour of his shoes.'

**4** Work with another student. One of you thinks of a man or woman in the class.
The other tries to find out who it is, in eight questions beginning 'Is he/she wearing. . .?'. Example:

'It's a man.' 'Is he wearing jeans?'
'No, he isn't.' 'Is he wearing glasses?'
'Yes, he is.' . . .

**5** Ask the teacher questions.

 'What's this called in English?'

 'What are these called?'

'How do you say boucles d'oreille in English?' 'Ear-rings.'
'How do you say rosa?' 'Pink.'
'How do you pronounce b-l-o-u-s-e?'

**6** Listen to the recording and answer the questions.

'Are you wearing a sweater?' 'Yes, I am.'
'Who's wearing brown shoes?' 'I am.'

RED
PINK
ORANGE
YELLOW
GREEN
BLUE
PURPLE
BROWN
BLACK
WHITE
LIGHT GREEN
DARK GREEN
LIGHT BLUE
DARK BLUE

# C I look like my father

## 1 Cover the text and listen. Look at the pictures. Who is speaking? Put the names with the pictures.

| Alice Ann Joe Philip Alice's father |
|---|
| Alice's mother Uncle George and family |
| Uncle Edward |

My name's Alice. I've got a sister (her name's Ann), and two brothers, Joe and Philip. We've all got fair hair and blue eyes, and we're all slim except Joe – he's very fat. Ann's very pretty, and she's got lots of boyfriends. I've only got one boyfriend: his name's Kevin, and he's very nice.

I look like my father – I've got his long nose and big mouth – but I've got my mother's personality. Joe and Phil both look more like Mum.

We've got two uncles and an aunt. Uncle George and Aunt Agnes have got three young children. Uncle Edward is only thirteen, so he hasn't got any children, but he's got a rabbit.

## 2 Who looks like who in your family? Examples:

'I look like my father.'
'My brother looks like me.'
'I've got my mother's eyes, but I've got my father's
    personality.'
'I don't look like my mother or my father.'

## 3

John and Sally have got children; so have Fred
    and Lucy.
Joe and Mary haven't got any children; nor have
    Pete and Anne.
The men have all got brothers and sisters; their
    wives haven't.
John, Joe, Sally and Mary have got green eyes; the
    others have got brown eyes.

**Work with another student. He or she is one of these eight people. Can you find out who? Ask three questions:**

Have you got any children?
Have you got any brothers or sisters?
What colour are your eyes?

## 4 Write sentences with *both* and *all*.
Examples:

*In my family we're all tall.*
*We all wear glasses.*
*My brothers are both architects.*
*My brother and I both look*
*   like our mother.*
*Carlos and I have both got dark hair.*

## 5 Look at the pictures again. You are one of these people: Ann, Joe, Philip, Alice's father, Alice's mother.
**Write about your family.**

# D  What a nice shirt!

## 1 Compliment other students.

What a / That's a — nice / pretty / lovely / beautiful — dress! / shirt! / jacket! / blouse! / etc.

What / Those are — nice / pretty / lovely / beautiful — ear-rings! / trousers! / shoes! / etc.

I like your — dress. / ear-rings. / etc.

That's a pretty dress!

Oh, thank you.

What a nice shirt!

Thank you very much.

What lovely ear-rings!

I like your new glasses.

Thank you.

Oh, thanks.

## 2 Work in groups. Show the other students photos of your family and friends, and talk about them.

This is my mother.

She's very pretty.

What nice eyes!

Who's that?

This is my brother. He's got blue eyes.

This is my sister—she's 23.

## 3 You are going on a holiday or business trip to another country. Write a letter to a person you don't know, asking him/her to meet you at the station, and giving a description of yourself. Here is an example.

1609 Burkitt Ave
Chicago, IL 60611

Mr G.D. Bell
Monument House
Castle Street
Edinburgh

September 12, 1984

Dear Mr Bell,

I am arriving at Waverley Station, Edinburgh, at 11.37 a.m. next Tuesday, September 17th. Can you meet me?

I am sorry that I have not got a photograph, but here is a description: I am 32, quite short with dark hair and a small beard. I have got blue eyes. I will be wearing a dark blue sweater and light grey trousers and black shoes.

I look forward to seeing you,

Yours sincerely,

Paul Sanders

## 4 Look at the summary on page 143 with your teacher.

# Revision and fluency practice

## A  Wanted for murder

**WANTED FOR MURDER**

PETER ROLAND ANDERSON
Aliases: PETER ROLAND, ANDREW ROWLANDS, ANDY PETERS.

**DESCRIPTION**
Age: 30, but looks younger
Height: 6'2" (1m 90)
Weight: 175 pounds (80kg)
Build: medium
Hair: black
Eyes: blue
Complexion: pale; scar under right eye
prominent nose
Nationality: British
Occupation: mechanic

**WARNING**
This man is armed and dangerous. If you see him, do not approach him, but contact the nearest police station immediately.

**1** Listening for information. Listen to the telephone conversations.
Who do you think saw Peter Anderson – the first caller (Mrs Collins), the second (Mr Sands), or the third (Mr Harris)?

**2** *Be* or *have*? Put in *am, are, is, have got,* or *has got.*

1. My sister ............ a very pretty cat.
2. How tall ............ you?
3. I don't know if they ............ any children.
4. It's very windy today – I ............ cold.
5. What colour ............ your car?
6. There ............ too many people in this room.
7. 'I ............ very hungry.'
8. 'I ............ some bread and cheese. Would you like some?'
9. You look as if you ............ thirsty. Have some beer.
10. You ............ beautiful eyes, Veronica.
11. ............ you married?
12. You ............ Italian, aren't you?
13. What time ............ the next train for Dublin?
14. My address ............ 13 Church Way, Llangollen.
15. She ............ tired after her journey.
16. How far ............ it from London to Rome?
17. I think they ............ artists. They look like artists.
18. You ............ your father's nose and mouth.
19. I ............ too much work and not enough free time.
20. 'Would you like a cold drink?' 'Yes, please. I ............ hot.'

**3** Listen to the recording. What is the *third* word in each sentence? (Contractions like *don't* count as two words.)

# B One way of getting money

how would you like it?

LLOYDS BANK 112

TUES 8 MAR

**1** Look at the picture and listen to the recording. How many differences can you find?

**2** Say these words.

1. thank   three   thirsty   third
2. the   this   then   mother

**Group 1 or group 2?**

| thing | Thursday | father | that | their |
|-------|----------|--------|------|-------|
| thousand | other | them | think | thirty |
| they | there | brother | these | thirteen |
| those | with | | | |

**3** Spell your name and address.

**4** Intonation. Look at these two conversations, and listen to the recording.

1. 'Cambridge 31453.' 'Mary?' 'No, this is Sally.'
2. 'What's your name?' 'Mary.'

In the first conversation, *Mary* is a question. The voice goes up. *Mary?*
In the second conversation, *Mary* is a statement. The voice goes down. *Mary.*

**Now listen to the words and expressions on the recording, and decide whether they are questions or statements. Write _Q_ or _S_ after the words.**

three o'clock ....Q.... London ....S....
Michael ..,....... Tuesday ........... a girl ...........
at the pub ........... a cigarette ...........
two pounds ........... Washington ...........
trinitrotoluene ...........

47

# C A rich 36-year-old dentist

## 1 Who is who?

Jane, Pete, Joe and Alice are from Birmingham, London, New York and Canberra (not in that order).

One is a doctor, one a dentist, one an artist and one a shop assistant.

Their ages are 19, 22, 36 and 47.

Apart from English, one of them speaks French, one German, one Greek and one Chinese.

Only one of them is tall, only one is good-looking, only one is rich, only one is dark. The tall one is 22.

One of them is a rich 36-year-old dentist from Canberra who speaks Chinese. What are the others?

**Ask your teacher questions. He or she can only answer *Yes* or *No*. Examples:**

*'Is Jane a dentist?' 'No.'*
*'Is the artist good-looking?' 'Yes.'*
*'Does Joe speak Chinese?' 'Yes.'*

| | | Alice | Joe | Pete | Jane |
|---|---|---|---|---|---|
| Appearance | Tall | | | | |
| | Good-looking | | | | |
| | Rich | | | | |
| | Dark | | | | |
| Age | 19 | | | | |
| | 22 | | | | |
| | 36 | | | | |
| | 47 | | | | |
| Profession | Doctor | | | | |
| | Dentist | | | | |
| | Artist | | | | |
| | Shop assistant | | | | |
| Home | Birmingham | | | | |
| | London | | | | |
| | New York | | | | |
| | Canberra | | | | |
| Languages | French | | | | |
| | German | | | | |
| | Greek | | | | |
| | Chinese | | | | |

## 2 Vocabulary revision. Add some more words to these lists.

1. chair, sofa, . . .
2. mother, brother, . . .
3. tomato, cheese, . . .
4. bathroom, living room, . . .
5. bank, post office, . . .
6. Spain, Australia, . . .
7. Monday, Friday, . . .
8. Italian, Chinese, . . .
9. cow, dog, . . .
10. I, she, . . .
11. my, her, . . .

## 3 Make sentences with *neither . . . nor*, as in the examples.

I am not tall and I am not short.
*'I am neither tall nor short.'*
Alex does not speak French and Rose does not speak French.
*'Neither Alex nor Rose speaks French.'*

1. I am not fair and I am not dark.
2. She is not at home and she is not in her office.
3. John is not fat, but he is not slim.
4. It is not true and it is not false.
5. I do not speak German and I do not speak French.
6. Compton has not got a bank or a post office.
7. John is not married and Peter is not married.
8. My mother does not smoke and my father does not smoke.

## 4 Make sentences with *neither . . . nor* about yourself and other people.

## 5 Pronounce these words.

brother son mother love money some once beautiful fruit usually
young touch cupboard     English women
many any friend sweater weather breakfast
night light right tight write eye quiet
daughter quarter water     half could
orange village     you're sure
child woman people tired wrong watch year
autumn enough aunt listen

48

# D Give me the money!

*REVISION EXERCISE: SKETCH*

**Work in groups of four to six.**
**Roles:** Mr Harris
Mrs Harris
Their child Alex
Bank manager
Wanted man or woman
Policeman or policewoman

**Write and practise a sketch, using the English you have learnt in Units 1–10.**
**In your sketch, you must use five of these sentences:**

First on the right, second on the left.
It's terrible.
It's foggy.
I'm sorry.
Two boys and a girl.
I quite like Picasso.
Tall, dark and good-looking.
What a pretty dress!
Hands up!
Give me the money!

# Personal history

## A He was born in London

**1** Close your book and listen. Try to remember as much as you can. Then look at the curriculum vitae. Listen again.

```
                CURRICULUM VITAE

NAME:              Philip George Hallow

DATE OF BIRTH:     21.3.47

PLACE OF BIRTH:    London

EDUCATION:         Highgate Hill School, London, 1959-1963.
                   GCE O level, 5 subjects.

FAMILY:            Father:  George David Hallow, retired
                            bus-driver.
                   Mother:  Alice  Emily  Hallow,  nee
                            Tomkins, housewife, died 1979.
                   Two sisters.

EMPLOYMENT:        1963-1976  Accounts clerk,
                   Imperial Furniture Company, York.
                   1976-1978 Unemployed.
                   1978-present  Area Manager,
                   Hartford Security Services Ltd., Bristol.

MARRIAGE:          Colette Andrews, 1970.

CHILDREN:          Two daughters, one son.
```

**2** Match these verbs from the text with their present tense forms.

| worked | died | married | went | left | became |
|---|---|---|---|---|---|
| marry | work | die | go | become | leave |

**3** Say these regular past tense verbs.

1. married   died   opened   played   lived
2. worked   liked   cooked   stopped   finished
3. started   hated   depended   painted   assisted

**4** Write your own curriculum vitae.

**5** Take another student's curriculum vitae and tell the class about it. Don't say the student's name!

> This person was born in Caracas in 1960. His mother worked as a nurse ...

> Is it Jaime?

# B  They didn't drink tea

**1** These pictures show life in the country in 1440. Make fifteen sentences about people who lived in Europe then; use *didn't*, *wasn't* and *weren't*. Examples:

'They didn't eat bananas.'
'They didn't drink tea.'
'They didn't have passports.'
'They didn't know about America.'
'Most people didn't live in cities.'
'Most people weren't very tall.'
'There wasn't any paper money.'

**3** Write seven sentences about changes in your life. Read one or two of them to the class. Examples:

*I didn't like cheese when I was a child, but now I do.*
*I played tennis when I was a girl, but now I don't.*
*We didn't have a colour television then, but now we've got one.*
*There weren't any pocket calculators then, but now there are millions of them.*

**2** How do you write regular past tenses? Here's how:

1. Most regular verbs:
   *work* + *ed* = *worked*; *listen* + *ed* = *listened*
2. Verbs ending in *e*:
   *live* + *d* = *lived*; *hate* + *d* = *hated*
3. Short verbs ending in consonant + vowel + consonant:
   *stop* + *ped* = *stopped*; *slim* + *med* = *slimmed*
4. Verbs ending in consonant + *y*:
   *study* + *ied* = *studied*

**Now write the past tenses of the regular verbs below.**

| | |
|---|---|
| arrive | live |
| cook | look |
| dance | start |
| shop | marry |
| remember | watch |

**4** Listen to two people talking about life in a farming village in England in the 1940s. Which of the following do they talk about?

electric light    heating    post office    car
radio    National Health System    clothes    shop

## C | Danced till half past one

**1** Match the present and past forms of these irregular verbs.

go tell get can do come hear (wake) have say know
(woke) could went heard said told came had did got knew

**2** Close your book and listen to the dialogue. See how much you can remember. Then read the dialogue and the text. Ask your teacher about new words.

## MAY 14 Tuesday

_Lovely_ time with Frank at the disco. Danced till half past one, then went to his place for a drink. We kissed a bit. F. wanted more, but I told him I didn't know him well enough yet. Got home at 3 a.m. again. Couldn't find my key, so climbed in through a window. V. tired this morning. Daddy asked a lot of stupid questions, as usual.

FATHER: What time did you come home last night, then, June?

JUNE: Oh, I don't know. About half past twelve, I think.

FATHER: Half past twelve? I didn't hear you.

JUNE: Well, I came in quietly. I didn't want to wake you up.

FATHER: You didn't go to that damned disco, did you?

JUNE: Disco, Daddy? Oh, no. You know I don't like loud music. No, I went to a folk concert with Alice and Mary. It was very good. There was one singer...

FATHER: Why did you come back so late? The concert didn't go on till midnight, did it?

JUNE: No, but we went to Alice's place and had coffee, and then we started talking about politics, you know. Alice's boyfriend – he's the President of the Students' Union Conservative Club...

**3** Find the differences. Example:

_June said (that) she went to a folk concert, but actually she went to a disco._

OR: _June told her father (that) she..._

**4** Ask some other students what they did _either_ yesterday _or_ at the weekend. Ask as many questions as possible. Examples:

'What time did you get up yesterday?'
'Did you come to school by bus?'
'Did you have a bath?'
'What did you have for breakfast?'

#  D  Who wrote to Alice?

## 1 Listen to the four speakers and fill in the table.

| NAME | AGE | BROTHERS | SISTERS | PLACE OF BIRTH | CHILDHOOD |
|------|-----|----------|---------|----------------|-----------|
| Steve Dixon | | | | Dartington<br>Darlington<br>Parlington | very happy<br>he quite enjoyed it<br>he liked it a lot |
| Adrian Webber | | | | India<br>England<br>Edinburgh | varied and quite happy<br>very unhappy<br>very happy |
| Lorna Higgs | | | | Austria<br>Oslo<br>Oxford | quite miserable<br>quite interesting<br>quite mixed, really |
| Sue Ward | | | | Tadcaster<br>Manchester<br>Hong Kong | very unhappy<br>very happy<br>varied and happy |

## 2 Four friends wrote letters on the same day.

Jane wrote to Alice.
Alice wrote to Mary.
Mary wrote to John.
John wrote to Jane.

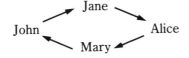

**Ask and answer questions about the letters.**
**Examples:**

*'Who wrote to Alice?'*  *'Jane did.' / 'Jane.'*
*'Who did Alice write to?'*  *'She wrote to Mary.' / 'Mary.'*

## 3 Make questions about these sentences.

1. Marilyn walked home from school with someone.
   Who *did she walk home* with?
   When *did she walk home from school*?
2. One of my women friends showed me some pictures.
   (When...? What sort...?)
3. They stopped to have lunch. (Who...? When...?
   Where...?)
4. Sandra went to work. (How...? What time...?)
5. There were some children at the party.
   (How many...?)
6. He started work at the same time every day.
   (Who...? What time...?)
7. He went on holiday with someone. (Who...?
   Who... with? Where...? When...?)
8. I heard someone in the street at midnight
   last night. (Who...?)
9. Susan's brother found something strange at
   the weekend. (What...? Where...?)
10. Matthew said he was with Sarah, but actually
    he wasn't. (Where...?)
11. Somebody climbed through a window. (Who...?
    When...?)

## 4 Choose one sentence for each cartoon.

'How was the holiday?'
'Happy birthday!'
'He's tired.'
'What's today?'
'Remember me from last night?'

## 5 Study the summary on page 144 with your teacher.

# Buying things

## A This one?

**1** Draw a picture of something. Ask and answer questions with other students.

*'What is this/that called in English?'*

**2** Draw a picture of two things; for example, two cats or two chairs. Ask and answer.

*'What are these/those called in English?'*

**3** Find these in the window.

| a ring | a spoon | some ear-rings | a glass | a watch | a box | a lamp | a Buddha | a teapot |

**4** Work in pairs: ask to see things, and answer.

**5** Say where things are in the window.

There's / There are — a / some — box, glasses, spoon, ear-rings, ring, watches, watch, teapot — in front of / behind / by / to the left of / to the right of — the lamp. / the red glasses. / the teapot. / some ear-rings. / the Buddha.

**6** Work in pairs: ask to see things again, and answer. Examples:

*'Could I see that box, please?'*
*'This one?'*
*'No, the one behind the teapot.'*

*'Could you show me those glasses, please?'*
*'These?'*
*'No, the red ones.'*

# B  Yellow doesn't suit me

**1** Match the sentences to their places in the conversations.

a. Can I help you?
b. I'm just looking.

a. Here's a lovely one.
b. What size?
c. Yes, I'm looking for a jumper.
d. Well, yellow doesn't really suit me.
   Have you got anything in blue?
e. Can I help you?

f. Can I try them on?
g. Here's a nice one in blue.
   And here's another one.
h. £13.99.
i. Yes, of course.
j. How much are they?

a. These are a bit small. Have
   you got them in a larger size?
b. Yes, these fit perfectly. I'll
   take them, please.
c. No, I'm afraid I haven't. Would
   you like to try these?
d. I'll just see.
e. Yes, please.

**2** Listen to the three conversations. Use your dictionary or ask your teacher about the new words. Then practise the customer's part in each conversation.

**3** Change things (clothes, colours, sizes) in the second conversation and practise the new conversation with another student.

**International clothing sizes**

| Women's clothes | | | | | | | |
|---|---|---|---|---|---|---|---|
| British | 10 | 12 | 14 | 16 | 18 | 20 | 22 |
| Continental | 38 | 40 | 42 | 44 | 46 | 48 | 50 |
| American | 8 | 10 | 12 | 14 | 16 | 18 | 20 |

| Women's shoes | | | | | | | |
|---|---|---|---|---|---|---|---|
| British | 3 | 4 | 5 | 6 | 7 | 8 | 9 |
| Continental | 35½ | 36½ | 38 | 39½ | 40½ | 42 | 43 |
| American | 4½ | 5½ | 6½ | 7½ | 8½ | 9½ | 10½ |

| Men's clothes | | | | |
|---|---|---|---|---|
| British | 37-38 | 39-40 | 41-42 | 43-44 |
| Continental | 94-97 | 99-102 | 104-107 | 109-112 |
| American | 38 | 40 | 42 | 44 |

| Men's shoes | | | | | | | |
|---|---|---|---|---|---|---|---|
| British | 7 | 8 | 9 | 10 | 11 | 12 | 13 |
| Continental | 41 | 42 | 43 | 44 | 45½ | 47 | 48 |
| American | 8 | 9 | 10 | 11 | 12 | 13 | 14 |

# C The next train to Oxford

**1** Listen, and complete the dialogues with your teacher's help. Then ask your teacher about the new words, or find them in your dictionary. Listen again.

1. TRAVELLER: ............................................ two
   singles ........... Norwich,
   .............
   CLERK: ........... £12.40, ...........
   TRAVELLER: Let's see, there's twelve, and
   ..........., twenty, ..........., forty.
   CLERK: ...................................
   TRAVELLER: ...................................
   NEXT
   TRAVELLER: Return ........... Cambridge,
   ............

2. TRAVELLER: What time is the next train to
   Oxford, please?
   CLERK: There's one at ..........., change
   at Didcot, arriving at Oxford at
   ..........., or there's a direct one
   at ..........., arriving at ...........
   TRAVELLER: Which platform for the ...........?
   CLERK: Platform ...........
   TRAVELLER: Thank you very much.

## INFORMATION

**BUREAU DE CHANGE**

3. CLERK: How would you like it?
   TRAVELLER: ...........?
   CLERK: How would you like it?
   TRAVELLER: ...................................
   ...................................?
   CLERK: How would you like your money?
   In tens?
   TRAVELLER: ...................................
   CLERK: Fifty, one, two, three and twenty
   pence. And here's your receipt.
   TRAVELLER: ...................................

| | |
|---|---|
| speak | understand |
| Thank | four fives |
| slowly | Pardon |

**2** Practise the traveller's part in each dialogue.

**3** In pairs, choose a dialogue and change the places and numbers. Practise the new dialogue.

**4** Which platform? Listen to the platform announcements and write the platform numbers.

a. Reading   c. Radley'   e. Swindon
b. Oxford   d. Goring

# D  Five hundred pounds for a month

**1** Listen to the recording of a man dictating a telegram over the telephone, and correct the following text.

**①Telemessage**                    British **TELECOM**

```
TELEMESSAGE
ROBINS
THE CODDARDS
CHILTERN
NEAR DIDCOT
OXFORDSHIRE

PLEASE SEND COMPLETE FIGURES FOR CLOTHING IMPORTS
TO JAMES PALATINE AS SOON AS POSSIBLE. TELEPHONE
ME TUESDAY MORNING AT 381 4155 TO DISCUSS GREEK
VISIT NEXT AUGUST.

REGARDS STEVE.
```

**2** Listen to the conversation and mark the stressed syllables.

A: What would you like to drink?
B: Beer, if you've got it.
A: I think so. Just a minute. Yes, here you are.
B: Thanks.
A: Cigarette?
B: No, thanks, I don't. How's the family?
A: They're OK. Peter's gone to the States for a month.
B: Oh, yes? Holiday?
A: Yes.
B: Isn't that expensive?
A: Not really. Five hundred pounds for a month including air fares and hotels. Without meals.
B: That's not bad.

**3** Ask your teacher how to pronounce words and expressions.

How do you pronounce t-h-o-u-g-h ?

Is this correct: ..........?

**4** Use these phrases to fill the blanks.

| how much | how many | too much | too many |
|---|---|---|---|
| | not much | not many | |

1. We've got ........... apples this year – we don't know where to put them all.
2. ........... people were there when I arrived, but a lot of Alice's friends came later.
3. There's a restaurant or a coffee shop – ........... time have you got?
4. There was ........... snow this year, but last year it snowed every day for a month.
5. I'd like to come, but I've just got ........... work at the moment.
6. ........... people came to the meeting on Thursday?
7. There's ........... toothpaste left – could you buy some?
8. I couldn't see the Queen very well; there were ........... people.
9. ........... music did they teach at your school?
10. There were ........... buses from my village to the city when I was a child.

**5** Look at the summary on page 145 with your teacher.

# Differences

## **A** I can sing, but I can't draw

**1** Which of these things can you do? Which of them can't you do?

**Example:** '*I can sing, but I can't draw.*'

| | | |
|---|---|---|
| play chess | speak German | |
| type | play the violin | drive |
| draw | run a mile | sing | play tennis |

**2** Can you swim / cook / play the piano / dance / go without sleep / sleep in the daytime? Ask two other people, and report their answers to the class. Make sentences with *but*.

'*Can you dance?*' '*Yes, I can.*'
'*No, I can't.*'
'*Diego can dance, but Alice can't.*'
'*Diego can dance, but he can't cook.*'

**3** In groups: find a person for each job. Tell the class about it. Example:

'*Preeda can do the first job. He can't play the guitar, but he can play the flute. He can cook and drive, and he likes children.*'

**4** Listen, and write *can* or *can't*.

Help us with our children and travel around the world. If you can play the guitar or another instrument, cook, and drive, phone Whitfield at 689 6328.

Travelling companion/driver required for American writer; speaking English, other languages. Chess player appreciated. Excellent pay. Write to Box 492, Newton Tribune.

Typist required, excellent pay, one week nights, 2 weeks days. Musician appreciated. Write to Box 635, Oxford OX6 82J

Take 2 Italian boys, 8 and 10, on holiday in June. Some cooking but no cleaning. Swimming, tennis, windsurfing. Very good pay. Phone Guidotti 278 3440 evenings.

# B  I can do anything better than you

| WHAT CAN THEY DO? | PLAY TENNIS | SING | COUNT | SPELL | RUN 100m | COOK | SPEAK ENGLISH |
|---|---|---|---|---|---|---|---|
| The Queen | ⊘⊘⊘⊘⊘ | ♪♪ | 1 2 3 | abcde | 43 secs | 🍳 | 3 words |
| The Prime Minister | ⊘⊘⊘ | ♪♪♪ | 1 2 | ab | 35 secs | 🍳🍳🍳 | 10 words |
| The Foreign Minister | ⊘ | ♪ | 1 | abc | 5 mins | – | – |
| The Minister of Education | ⊘⊘ | ♫♫♫ | 3 1 4 2 | a | – | 🍳🍳 | 1 word |
| The Minister of Finance | ⊘⊘⊘⊘ | ♪♪♪♪ | 0 | abcd | 22 secs | 🍳🍳🍳🍳🍳 | 400 words |

**1** **True or false? Look at the table.**

1. The Queen can spell very well.
2. The Foreign Minister can count quite well.
3. The Minister of Education can't run.
4. The Minister of Finance can't speak English.
5. The Prime Minister can't count.
6. The Queen can cook better than the Minister of Finance.
7. The Minister of Education can sing better than the Queen.
8. The Prime Minister can run faster than the Minister of Education.
9. The Minister of Education can spell better than the Foreign Minister.
10. The Queen can spell better than all the others.

**2** True or false? Listen to the recording.

**3** Make some sentences with *better than*. Example:

*'I can cook better than my sister.'*

**4** Talk about now and when you were younger; use *than* and *but*.

*'When I was younger I couldn't cook at all, but now I can cook quite well.'*

*'I was good at maths when I was younger, but I'm not now.'*

*'I could swim better when I was younger than I can now.'*

*'My father can speak Spanish better now than he could when I was younger.'*

*'I'm better at running now than I was when I was younger.'*

**5** In teams: try to remember other students' sentences. One point for each correct one.

> Michel can ski better now than he could when he was younger.

> You're right./ I'm afraid you're wrong.

**6** Say these words after the recording or your teacher.

1. am    cat    back    hand    bad
2. came    late    wake    rain    made
3. car    last    glasses    bath    half
4. saw    tall    walk    talk    all

**7** 1, 2, 3 or 4? Decide how to pronounce these and then check with your teacher or the recording.

a. past ...3......    f. part
b. page              g. pass
c. map               h. Spain
d. bag               i. law
e. ball              j. tape

**8** Listen to the song.

## C I'm much taller than my mother

LONGER

smaller

TALLER

**cold**er

*Faster*

BIGGER

**1** Look at the list of adjectives. Can you see any rules? What are the comparative and superlative of these words?

long  *longer   longest*
dark          hungry
cold          nice
near          intelligent
big           expensive

| ADJECTIVE | COMPARATIVE | SUPERLATIVE |
|---|---|---|
| 1. old | older | oldest |
| young | younger | youngest |
| short | shorter | shortest |
| tall | taller | tallest |
| cheap | cheaper | cheapest |
| cool | cooler | coolest |
| 2. fat | fatter | fattest |
| thin | thinner | thinnest |
| 3. happy | happier | happiest |
| easy | easier | easiest |
| 4. late | later | latest |
| fine | finer | finest |
| 5. good | better | best |
| bad | worse | worst |
| far | farther | farthest |
| 6. interesting | more interesting | most interesting |
| beautiful | more beautiful | most beautiful |
| difficult | more difficult | most difficult |

**2** Compare people you know.

A is (much) taller        than B.
    (a bit)  shorter
             older
             younger
             thinner
             etc.

*'I'm much taller than my mother.'*
*'Mario's a bit older than his brother.'*

**In your family, who is the oldest / the youngest / the shortest / the best at English?**

**3** Compare countries (warm/cold/big/small/ cheap/expensive/noisy/quiet) or cars (big/small/ fast/slow/expensive/cheap/comfortable/ economical/good).

*'Japan is much more expensive than Greece.'*
*'A Volkswagen is much cheaper than a Mercedes.'*

**4** Compare your liking for steak, chicken, trout, pizza and curry. Which do you like best?

*'I like steak better than pizza.'*
*'I like trout best.'*

**5** Compare Einstein, Chaplin, Cleopatra, Getty, de Gaulle, John Lennon, Samson (intelligent, rich, funny, strong, beautiful, tall, interesting).

*'Getty was richer than Einstein.'*
*'Samson was the strongest.'*

# D The same or different?

## 1 The same or different? (Use your dictionary.)

1. 7 × 12 and 3 × 28
2. Britain and England
3. Holland and The Netherlands
4. The USSR and Russia
5. Peking and Beijing
6. three o'clock and 15.00
7. a café and a pub
8. handsome and pretty
9. a woman and a wife
10. a pen and a pencil
11. 4,718 and 4.718
12. a cooker and a cook
13. a typewriter and a typist
14. a telephone number and a phone number

**Write three sentences with *the same as* and three with *different from*.**
**Examples:**

*Three o'clock in the afternoon is the same as 15.00.*
*A café is different from a pub.*

## 2 Compare some of these people and things. Use *(not) as... as...*
**Examples:**

*I'm as good-looking as Robert Redford.*
*A Volkswagen is not as quiet as a Rolls-Royce.*

I/me   Robert Redford   a Volkswagen
a Rolls-Royce   the President   Bach
an elephant   a cat   Canada
rock music   Kenya   a piano

tall   heavy   good-looking
strong   old   fast   economical
cold   warm   cheap   expensive   big
noisy   quiet   comfortable
intelligent   nice

## 3 As or than?

1. I can sing better ............ you.
2. Elizabeth's much taller ............ her brother.
3. I'm ............ old ............ my teacher.
4. Your eyes are the same colour ............ mine.
5. Germany is bigger ............ Switzerland.
6. Your problems are not ............ important ............ mine.

## 4 Listen to the recording. How many words are there in each sentence? What are they? (Contractions like *I'm* count as two words.)

## 5 Work in groups. In each group, make a detailed comparison between two people, or two countries, or two cars, or two other things. Find as many things to say as possible. Write down all the things you think of.

## 6 Look at the summary on page 145 with your teacher.

*"How d'you mean I'm as fit as a man of thirty—I am thirty!"*

# Some history

## A 91 million years ago

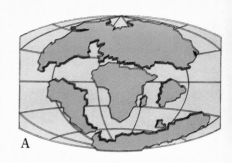

**1** Put the pictures in order by reading the text. You can use a dictionary or ask your teacher for help.

A long time ago, Africa was not far from South America. In fact, 300 million years ago all the land on earth was only one big continent, called 'Pangaea'.

Very slowly, Pangaea separated into two parts, and the future continents began to move towards their places. But until 160 million years ago South America, Africa, India, Australia and Antarctica were still only one huge land mass ('Gondwanaland'). North America, Europe and Asia together made the other super-continent ('Laurasia').

Then Gondwanaland and

Laurasia also began to divide. Seas started to spread between the new continents. This was a slow process: Africa and South America only finished separating 91 million years ago.

Some strange results of land mass movements:
1. There is a diamond deposit that starts in Africa, stops on the west coast, and begins again in South America.
2. Mountains in Norway, Scotland, Greenland and the north-east US all belong to the same mountain chain.

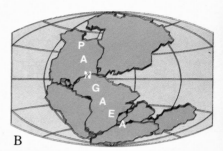

**2** When did it happen? Match the two halves of each sentence. Example:

*'Julius Caesar invaded Britain about 2,000 years ago.'*

The last dinosaurs died      about 3½ million years ago.
The French Revolution happened      about 2,000 years ago.
Julius Caesar invaded Britain      about 400 years ago.
The Great Pyramid was built      about 500 years ago.
Columbus discovered America      about 4,500 years ago.
Europeans discovered Australia      about 200 years ago.
The first people lived on earth      about 70 million years ago.

**3** Ask and answer questions with *ago.* Example:

*'How long ago was World War II?' 'About 40 years ago.'*

New Year's Day      4.00 a.m.      the beginning of this class      last Tuesday
World War I      your first English lesson      etc.

**4** Fill each blank with a word from the text in Exercise 1.

I don't live with my husband now; we ............ six months ago. I ............ see him occasionally, but we don't want to live together again.

It is difficult to say when our problems ............ Slowly, life became more and more uncomfortable; even very small problems looked ............ to us. We are both happier now that we have ............ living together.

It was not difficult to ............ our belongings into mine and his, but I was a bit upset the day I ............ my things into my new flat. It meant an important part of my life was really ............ .

**B** **Where was Galileo born?**

**1** Match four of the phrases with each picture. You can use a dictionary.

A
born in Paris, France and Warsaw, Poland
born in Annam, Viet Nam
born in Atchison, Kansas, USA
born in Pisa, Italy

B
student in Saigon
student at the University of Pisa
student at Columbia University, New York
professors of physics at the Sorbonne, Paris

C
mathematician, astronomer and physicist
politician and poet
physicists and teachers
pilot and writer

D
first woman to fly a plane across the Atlantic
people who discovered radium
founder of the People's Republic of Viet Nam
man who discovered sunspots

Galileo,
1564-1642

Amelia Earhart,
1898-?1937

Ho Chi Minh,
1892-1969

Marie and Pierre Curie,
1867-1934 and 1859-1906

**2** Close your book. Ask and answer questions about the four people. Examples:

*'Where was Amelia Earhart born?'*
*'In Kansas, I think. What did Ho Chi Minh do?'*
*'He was a politician. Who discovered sunspots?'*
*'I don't remember. The Curies?'*

**3** Listen, and match the names with the phrases.

1. Galileo
2. Earhart
3. Ho Chi Minh
4. The Curies

a. Nobel prize
b. lorry driver
c. famous for lectures
d. photographer

**4** Ask and answer questions about famous people in the past. Examples:

*'Who was the first man to walk on the moon?'*
*'Neil Armstrong.'*
*'Who was Simon Bolivar?'*
*'The founder of Bolivia.'*

**5** 1. One student thinks of a famous person, or a group of famous people, from the past.
2. The student says one affirmative and two negative sentences, for example:
*'This was a woman. She wasn't American. She wasn't a writer.'*
3. The other students try to guess who it is by asking questions with yes/no answers; for example:
*'Was she European? Was she married? Did she work in America?'*

# C America invades Britain!

**1** **Put the pictures in the correct order. Only use your dictionary for the important words.**

In 1778 the British had the strongest navy in the world. They laughed at the small navy of their American colonies, who were fighting Britain for their independence.

One American captain decided to show the British that size was not everything. Here is what happened:

On the night of April 24, 1778, Captain John Paul Jones silently brought the American ship *Ranger* into Whitehaven harbour on the west coast of England. As soon as he arrived, he took a group of his men to a local inn, broke into it, and had a drink with them.

Then they went back to the harbour and began their work. Some of them went to the fort and put the guns out of order; others began burning British ships. The British sailors finally woke up, and put up a good fight, but they lost to Jones and his men.

Captain Jones was pleased, but not completely satisfied. So he sailed to the nearby Scottish coast and went to the home of the Earl of Selkirk. Jones and his men put all of the Earl's silverware onto the *Ranger* to take back to America! The British did not laugh so much about America's navy after Jones' visit.

**2** **Irregular verbs: match the present and past forms.**

| began | made | brought | (took) | broke | put | lost |
|-------|------|---------|--------|-------|-----|------|
| put | bring | lose | make | (take) | begin | break |

**3** **Read the text below, and put one of these words or expressions into each blank.**

| after | at midnight | finally | as soon as |
|-------|-------------|---------|------------|
| about | dancing | and then | on the night of |
| others | sang | so | some |
| went | began | | some of them |

.................................... December 31st, we invited .................................... friends to a New Year's Eve party. .................................... the first guests arrived, we offered them drinks, .................................... we put on some music.
.................................... half an hour there were .................................... thirty people in our small flat. ....................... ........................... to dance; .................................... just went on talking, eating and drinking. ............................... we all joined hands and .................................... an old Scottish song called 'Auld Lang Syne'; then we went on .................................... .

At seven o'clock in the morning there were still eight people left, .................................... we had breakfast. .................................... the last guest went home, and we .................................... to bed.

**4** **Write a story using at least five of the words or expressions from Exercise 3. You can write about a journey, a holiday, a party, a nice birthday, etc.**

# D Who? How? What? Where? Which?

## 1 History quiz. Take turns answering the questions.

1. How did Louis Blériot travel from France to England in 1909?
2. Who killed President Kennedy?
3. Who made the 'Long March' in China?
4. What animals did Hannibal take across the Alps on his invasion of Italy?
5. How many wives did King Henry VIII have?
6. Where was Jesus Christ born?
7. Copernicus disagreed with Ptolemy. What about?
8. Who first sent radio signals across the Atlantic?
9. Where was 'New Amsterdam'?
10. Who discovered penicillin?
11. Who starred in the film *The Sound of Music*?
12. Which of these were members of the 'Marx Brothers': Harpo, Karl, Groucho, Choco?
13. Who wrote the James Bond novels?
14. What were the names of the Beatles?
15. Which famous painter cut off his ear?
16. Which sport was Pele famous for?
17. These people were (or are) famous for the same sport. What is it? Jesse Owens, Abebe Bikila, Grete Waitz, Sebastian Coe.
18. Who built the Eiffel Tower?

## 2 Read these sentences to another student.

1. **Who** was at the **of**fice **when** you ar**ri**ved? **No**body **was.**
2. Were **Paul** and **Ann** at the **par**ty? **They weren't**, but the **Nel**sons **were.**
3. His **mo**ther and **fa**ther were **both doc**tors.
4. **Ein**stein was **A**merican, but he **was**n't **born** in A**me**rica.

## 3 Stressed or not? Underline *was* and *were* where they are stressed. Then read the sentences to another student.

1. Were **a**ny of the **chil**dren **there**? **Kev**in and **Ma**tthew were, but the **o**thers **weren't**.
2. **Ann was**n't at **home** when I **got there**.
3. **Who** was the **first per**son to **swim** the **Eng**lish **Chan**nel?
4. **I** was in Ja**pan** when my **fa**ther **died**.

## 4 Put the verbs into the past tense.

1. My sister ............ me with my homework. (help)
2. The school year ............ three months ago. (begin)
3. When I was younger I ............ mushrooms. (hate)
4. My brother never ............ football when he was a child. (play)
5. It ............ us three hours to get home on Friday. (take)
6. I ............ my passport in Barcelona once. (lose)
7. She always ............ about her weight when she was younger. (worry)
8. The jacket ............ him perfectly. (fit)
9. My car ............ making a terrible noise two days ago. (start)
10. Her grandmother ............ ten children. (have)

## 5 Read these questions about Thomas Morley, an English musician. Then listen to the recording and try to answer the questions.

1. When was Morley born?
2. Who was the Queen at the time?
3. What was the name of Morley's writer friend?
4. What was the date of Morley's own book?
5. Was Morley's best music dramatic or light?

## 6 Look at the summary on page 146 with your teacher.

# Personal information

## A  Ages, heights and weights

**1** How old do you think the buildings are? Example:

*'I think building 1 is about 400 years old.'*

How old is your house?

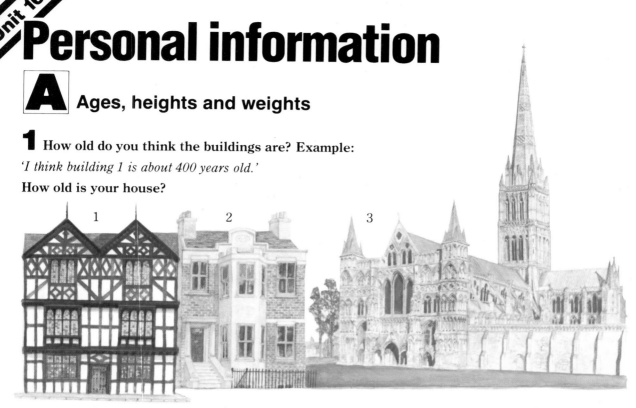

1    2    3

**2** How old do you think the people are? Examples:

*'I think Mark is six months old.'*
*'I think Mike is forty (years old).'*

| Mark | Thomas | Kate | Stuart | Mike | Ann |

**3** Look at the chart and make sentences. Example:

*'Thomas is five feet six (inches tall), and he weighs 130 pounds.'*

|        | HEIGHT   | WEIGHT |
| ------ | -------- | ------ |
| Mark   | 2ft 1in  | 14lbs  |
| Thomas | 5ft 6ins | 130lbs |
| Kate   | 5ft 4ins | 125lbs |
| Stuart | 5ft 10ins| 180lbs |
| Mike   | 6ft 2ins | 200lbs |
| Ann    | 5ft 1in  | 112lbs |

**4** Make sentences about yourself and other people. Examples:

*'I'm five feet six inches tall.'*
*'My husband is six feet tall.'*
*'My father weighs about 190lbs.'*
*'My mother's sixty-six, but she looks older.'*
*'I'm thirty-four, and I look my age.'*
*'I'm over twenty-one.'*

**5** Ask some other students.

*'How old/tall are you?'*
*'How much do you weigh?'*

**6** Listen to the recording. Some English-speaking people are trying to guess other people's ages and heights.

**7** Describe your dream man/woman. How old is he/she? How tall? How much does he/she weigh? What does he/she look like?

| 1 inch = 2½cm |
| 12 inches = 1 foot (30cm) |
| 1lb = about 450gm |
| 2.2lbs = 1 kilogram |

# B You look shy

## 1
What do they do? Look at the pictures. The six people are: *a criminal, a poet, a footballer, a businessman, a scientist* and *a politician.* Discuss who does what.
Examples:

*'I think C is a poet.' 'I don't
    agree. I think he's a criminal.'
'D looks like a scientist.' 'No, C
    looks more like a scientist.'*

## 2
What are they like? Look at the pictures and discuss the people's personalities.
Useful words:

| | | |
|---|---|---|
| kind | shy | sensitive |
| self-confident | | intelligent |
| stupid | bad-tempered | |
| calm | friendly | nervy |

Examples:

*'What is A like, do you think?'
    'I think she's shy.'
'I think C looks rather friendly.'
    'I don't agree. I think he looks
    very bad-tempered.'*

## 3
Say some things about yourself and other people. Ask about other people. Examples:

*'I look shy, but I'm not.'
'What's your sister like?' 'She's
    rather bad-tempered.'*

## 4 Read your sign with a dictionary. Is it true?

**Aries** (21/3 - 20/4): energetic, bossy, often bad-tempered, warm, generous, sensitive, artistic.
**Taurus** (21/4 - 21/5): hardworking, calm, friendly, interested in business, money, friends and family.

**Gemini** (22/5 - 21/6): clever, witty, very talkative, changeable, interested in books, people and ideas.
**Cancer** (22/6 - 23/7): humorous, conservative, often happy, anxious, shy. Interested in history.
**Leo** (24/7 - 23/8): proud, bossy, independent; either very tidy or very untidy; passionate and generous.
**Virgo** (24/8 - 23/9) practical, punctual, critical, hard-working, perfectionist. Interested in nature.

**Libra** (24/9 - 23/10): friendly, energetic (but also lazy), pleasant, argumentative. Interested in sport, animals.
**Scorpio** (24/10 - 22/11): brave, sometimes violent, extremist, possessive, passionate. Often very religious.
**Sagittarius** (23/11 - 21/12): talkative, self-confident, cheerful. Interested in sport, travel, living dangerously.
**Capricorn** (22/12 - 20/1): conservative, polite, serious, sociable but shy. Interested in home, politics, people.
**Aquarius** (21/1 - 19/2): tolerant, sociable but unstable. Interested in sport and politics. Often brilliant or mad.
**Pisces** (20/2 - 20/3): sensitive, emotional, imaginative, artistic, depressive. Very interested in themselves.

It's not true! I'm not talkative! I'm not talkative! I'm r

# C When is your birthday?

## 1 Listen to the conversation and answer the teacher's questions.

JANET: Happy birthday, Shirley.
SHIRLEY: Oh, thanks, Janet.
JANET: How old are you, then?
SHIRLEY: Never mind. Look at my new ring.
JANET: Oooooh! Shirley! It's beautiful! Is it a birthday present?
SHIRLEY: Yes. David gave it to me.
JANET: What's he like, then?
SHIRLEY: Oh, he's really nice, Jan.
JANET: Yes, but what's he *like*?
SHIRLEY: Well, he's *terribly* shy. But very interesting when he gets talking. And he's tall, dark and very good-looking. *I* think so, anyway.
JANET: What does he do?
SHIRLEY: He works in a bank. Assistant manager.
JANET: Oh, nice.
SHIRLEY: Yes. He's just got a new car.
JANET: Oh, yes? What sort?
SHIRLEY: A big red Mercedes.
JANET: Ooh! How old is he?
SHIRLEY: Twenty-eight. Twenty-nine next Tuesday.
JANET: What does your mother . . .

## 2 Fill in the missing numbers.

| | | |
|---|---|---|
| 1st   first | 13th ............ | 31st ............ |
| 2nd ............ | 14th ............ | 40th ............ |
| 3rd ............ | 18th ............ | 52nd ............ |
| 4th ............ | 20th   twentieth | 63rd ............ |
| 5th ............ | 21st   twenty-first | 70th ............ |
| 11th ............ | 22nd   twenty-second | 99th ............ |
| 12th   twelfth | 30th ............ | 100th ............ |

## 3 Pronounce the names of the months.

**January**   **February**   **March**   April   **May**
**June**   July   **August**   September   October
November   December

## 4 Ask and answer.

*'What's the eighth month?' 'August.'*

## 5 When is your birthday? Examples:

*'My birthday is on March the twenty-first.'*
*'My birthday is today.' 'Happy birthday!'*

**Now listen to some people saying when their birthdays are. Two of them have got the same birthday. When is it?**

## 6 Dates.

| Write | Say |
|---|---|
| Jan 14, 1983 | January the fourteenth, nineteen eighty-three |
| April 5, 1482 | April the fifth, fourteen eighty-two |
| December 9, 1793 | December the ninth, seventeen ninety-three |

**Say these dates:**

Jan 14, 1978    May 17, 1936    Dec 30, 1983
Aug 3, 1066    Oct 10, 1906    Mar 3, 1860
Sept 21, 1980    July 20, 1840    April 1, 1900

## 7 Vocabulary revision. Some students will draw things from Units 1–15. Say what they are. Examples:

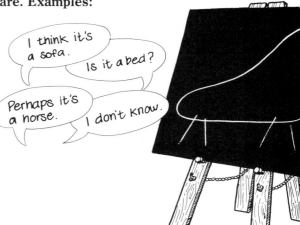

I think it's a sofa.
Is it a bed?
Perhaps it's a horse.
I don't know.

# D  Have you got a cat?

**1** Make two questions: one with *a* and one with *any*.

> Have you got | a / any | English books  bicycle  children  piano  animals  British money  guitar  TV  calculator  cat  jazz records  gold watch  perfume  car  American friends | ?

**2** Make two 'follow-up' questions. Examples:

*'Have you got a car?' 'Yes, I have.'*
*'What sort of car? What colour is it?'*

*'Have you got a guitar?' 'Yes, I have.'*
*'Can you play it? How often do you play?'*

*'Have you got a calculator?' 'Yes, I have.'*
*'Where did you buy it? Was it expensive?'*

**3** Ask your questions. Make a note of the answers.

**4** Report to the class. Examples:

*'Four students have got bicycles.'*
*'Two people have got some jazz records.'*
*'There are three students with children.'*
*'Only one student has got an animal.'*
*'Nobody has got any British money.'*
*'Maria hasn't got a bicycle.'*
*'27 per cent of the students have got cars.'*
*'Heinz has got a guitar. He can't play it.'*

**5** Have you got everything you want? No?
What haven't you got? Examples:

*'I haven't got a raincoat.'*
*'I haven't got any nice clothes.'*
*'I haven't got enough books.'*

**6** Pronunciation. Say these words after the
recording or after your teacher.

1. sit    in    big
2. wine    five    night    right
3. first    shirt

Now decide how to pronounce these words. Are
they in group 1, 2 or 3? Check with your
teacher or the recording.

a. girl     e. white    i. fin     m. bright
b. like     f. skirt    j. bird    n. excite
c. arrive   g. light    k. stir    o. ride
d. tights   h. with     l. slight  p. skip

**7** Look at the summary on page 147 with
your teacher.

69

# Ordering and asking

## A  I'll have roast beef

**1** Put the sentences in order.

1

'Yes, sir. Over here, by the window.'
'Have you got a table for two?'

2

'How would you like your steak?'
'Oh, all right, then. I'll have a rump
  steak.'
'I'll start with soup, please, and
  then I'll have roast beef.'
'I'm sorry, madam, there's no more
  roast beef.'
'Rare, please.'

3

'Vegetables, sir?'
'Chicken for me, please.'
'A few mushrooms and a green
  salad, please.'
'And for you, sir?'

4

'Certainly, madam.'
'Could I have a lager, please?'
'Would you like something to drink?'
'I'll have a lager too. And could you
  bring me some water?'

5

'A bit tough. The vegetables are
  nice.'
'Not too bad. What about your
  steak?'
'How's the chicken?'

6

'Is everything all right?'
'Very good.'
'Oh yes, excellent, thank you.'

'Could you bring us the bill, please?'
'No, sir.'
'Can I give you a little more coffee?'
'No, thank you.' 'Yes, please.'
'Is service included?'

7

8

9

**2** Listen to the conversation and practise the pronunciation. Then practise the conversation
in pairs. Make up your own 'restaurant' conversations.

70

# B Could you lend me some sugar?

**1** Read the story and complete the conversation.
Practise the complete conversation with a partner.

Excuse me, my name's Alan. I live downstairs.

Hello.

I'm sorry to trouble you, but could you lend me some sugar?

Yes, of course. Just a minute.

Here you are.

Thanks very much.

**2** Match the questions and answers. You can find more than one answer to each question.

QUESTIONS
1. Sorry to trouble you. Could you lend me some bread?
2. Could you lend me a dictionary?
3. Could you show me some black sweaters, please?
4. Excuse me. Have you got a light, please?
5. Could you possibly lend me your car for half an hour?
6. Could I borrow your keys for a moment?
7. Could I borrow your umbrella, please?
8. Have you got a cigarette?

ANSWERS
a. Yes, of course. Here you are.
b. Yes, of course. Just a minute.
c. I'm sorry. I need it/them.
d. I'm afraid I haven't got one.
e. I'm afraid I haven't got any.
f. Sorry, I don't smoke.
g. Sorry, I'm afraid I can't.

**3** Ask the teacher the names of some of
your possessions. Examples:

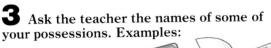

'What's this?'

'What's this called
in English, please?'

'Is this a pen
or a pencil?'

'Is this a lighter?'

**4** Ask other students to lend, give or show you things. Example:

'Could you lend me your watch?' 'I'm sorry, I need it.'

# C Something to drink?

## 1 Listen to the dialogue and see what you can remember.

MARY: Hello, John. What a surprise! Come in.
JOHN: Thank you, Mary.
MARY: Sit down. Would you like something to drink? Beer? Scotch? A cup of tea?
JOHN: Yes, thanks. Perhaps some Scotch. With a little water, please. I'm quite thirsty.
MARY: It's a hot day... Here you are. Help yourself to water.
JOHN: Thanks.
MARY: Can I give you something to eat? A piece of apple pie? Some biscuits?
JOHN: Er, no, nothing to eat, thanks. I'm not hungry. Mary, can I talk to you for a few minutes? I've got this letter from Sue. She...

## 2 A little or a few?

1. Could you bring us ........... water?
2. Could you possibly lend me ........... potatoes until tomorrow?
3. There's ........... cheese in the fridge, if you're hungry.
4. Have you got ........... minutes? I'd like to talk to you.
5. I need ........... money. Can you help me?
6. I'm going to France for ........... days next week.

## 3 Put in of if necessary.

1. Would you like a few ........... biscuits?
2. Can I give you a piece ........... apple pie?
3. Could I have a cup ........... tea?
4. I'd like some ........... cheese and a glass ........... milk, please.
5. Could you give me a lot ........... potatoes – I'm hungry.
6. And I'd like a little ........... salad, please.
7. I've got too many ........... letters to write.
8. I've got about two hundred ........... letters to write.
9. Please don't give me much ........... Scotch – I just want a little.
10. My sister's got lots ........... boyfriends.

## 4 Work in pairs. Offer your partner something to eat and something to drink.

Would you like

something to eat?
a piece of...?
a little...?
some...?
a few...?
something to drink?
a cup of...?
a glass of...?

Thank you very much.
Yes, I would.
Yes, please.
A Coke, please.
Just a little, please.

No, thank you.
I'm not hungry, thanks.
I'm not thirsty, thank you.

# D | I like Alice; Alice likes me

| SUBJECT | OBJECT | POSSESSIVE | EXAMPLES |
|---------|--------|------------|----------|
| I | me | my | I like Alice. Alice likes **me**. There's **my** house. |
| you | you | your | Are **you** married? Thank **you**. What's **your** name? |
| he | him | his | **He** works in London. Give **him** your phone number. **His** wife is American. |
| she | her | her | **She** is a doctor. I like **her**. **Her** husband travels a lot. |
| it | it | its | **It**'s raining. I don't like **it**. That's a pretty cat – what's **its** name? |
| we | us | our | **We** usually get up at seven. Please show **us** some rings. **Our** flat is on the sixth floor. |
| you | you | your | Do **you** both smoke? Can I help **you**? What is **your** address? |
| they | them | their | Where are **they**? Can I try **them** on? The children are with **their** aunt in Manchester. |

**1** Put in the right word.

1. Could you show ............ that ring? (I/me/my)
2. I can't remember ............ name. (she/her)
3. When is ............ birthday? (you/your)
4. I don't want to give ............ my name. (he/him/his)
5. Andrew lost ............ wallet yesterday. (he/him/his)
6. I like ............ very much. (she/her)
7. ............ are both tall and dark. (We/Us/Our)
8. So are ............ children. (we/us/our)
9. Could you give ............ your name? (we/us/our)
10. Can you help ............? (we/us/our)
11. Can I try ............ on? (they/them/their)
12. How much are ............? (they/them/their)

**2** Is the structure polite or rude? Read these sentences and write: P (polite) or R (rude).

1. Give me your pen. ...*R*.......
2. Excuse me. Could you lend me your pen? ...*P*.......
3. Please lend me your pen. ...*R*.......
4. Give me a light, please.
5. Excuse me. Could you give me a light, please?
6. Excuse me. Could I look at your newspaper?
7. Have you got a light, please?
8. Could you lend me £5 for a couple of days, John?

**3** Is the intonation polite or rude? Listen; mark the sentences P or R. Then say them politely.

1. Could you lend me a pen, please?
2. Have you got a light, please?
3. Can you tell me the time, please?
4. Could I look at your newspaper for a moment?
5. Could you send this to my address in Tokyo?
6. Can you show me some sweaters, please?

**4** Say these sentences; compare the rhythm.

☐ ☐☐ ☐
A. Where do you live?

☐ ☐ ☐ ☐
B. These books are cheap.

☐ ☐ ☐ ☐
C. I like the sea.

**Now group these sentences according to their rhythm: A, B, or C.**

What do you think?  Jane works in Greece.
She drinks a lot.  He went in May.
Green eyes are nice.  I've got some wool.
First on the right.  Right at the top.
Five pounds of meat.  A cup of tea.

**5** Say these words after the recording or after your teacher.

1. not    job    stop    lost
2. home    phone    no    wrote
3. more    born    short    or

**1, 2 or 3? Decide how to pronounce these words and check with your teacher or the recording.**

a. on      e. bored   i. dog      m. road
b. sport   f. those   j. go       n. know
c. note    g. forty   k. morning  o. snow
d. got     h. hotel   l. clock    p. boat

**6** Look at the summary on page 148 with your teacher.

# The present

## A

**What's happening?**

Hello, darling...Yes... Are you having a good time?...How's your mother?...What?...What do you mean, 'what's happening?'...Oh, the noise...Yes, it's the TV – I'm watching something good on the TV...What?...

**1** Who is the man on the phone talking to? What does she think is happening in the room? What is really happening? Examples:

*'Some people are dancing.'*
*'A man is lying on the floor.'*

**2** Memory test. Who is doing what? Work in pairs: one student closes his/her book, and the other asks questions about the picture. Examples:

*'What is the woman in the red dress doing?'*
*'What is the man with glasses doing?'*

**3** What do you think your wife/husband/ father/mother/boyfriend/girlfriend/boss etc. is doing at this moment?

*'I think my boyfriend's working. My wife's shopping. John's probably getting up.'*

**4** Mime an action. The others will try to say what you're doing.

You're drinking.

I think you're shaving.

I don't know what he's doing.

# B The Swan-Walter Universal Holiday Postcard Machine

**1** It's easy to write holiday postcards! Write one now and send it to a friend.

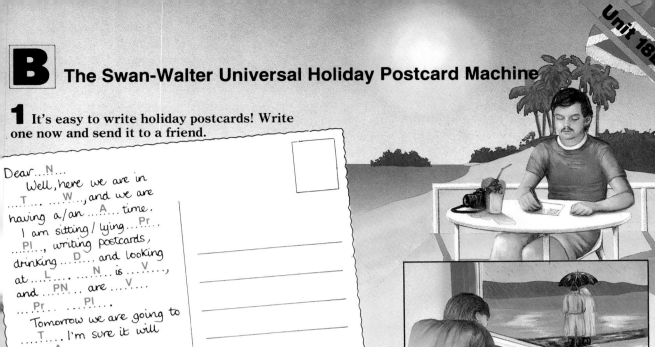

Dear ...N...
Well, here we are in ...T... ...W..., and we are having a/an ...A... time. I am sitting / lying ...Pr... ...Pl..., writing postcards, drinking ...D... and looking at ...L... ...N... is ...V..., and ...PN... are ...V... ...Pr... ...Pl.... Tomorrow we are going to ...T.... I'm sure it will be ...A... Wish you were here, Love, ...N...

POSTCARD DICTIONARY

**N** *(name)*
John
Mary
Alexandra
Mother
etc.

**T** *(town, city, village)*
Rome
Manchester
Honolulu
etc.

**W** *(weather)*
The sun is shining
It is raining
It is snowing
There is a hurricane
etc.

**A** *(adjective)*
wonderful     terrible
beautiful     awful
lovely        horrible
exciting      catastrophic
interesting   boring
magnificent   etc.

**Pr** *(preposition)*
in
on
at
under
by
near
opposite
etc.

**Pl** *(place)*
my room
their room
the bar
the beach
a café
a tree
a mountain
etc.

**D** *(drink)*
coffee
beer
wine
etc.

**L** *(things to look at)*
the sea
the mountains
the tourists
the rain
the sheep
etc.

**V** *(verb)*
shopping
sightseeing
sleeping
drinking beer
dancing
playing cards
having a bath
etc.

**PN** *(plural noun)*
the children
Mummy and Daddy
George and Sue
etc.

**2** Spelling. Make the *-ing* form.

1. sing *singing*        work ..........
   play *playing*        start ..........
   stand ..........       eat ..........
   read ..........        go ..........

2. make *making*         dance ..........
   smoke *smoking*       drive ..........
   write ..........       like ..........

3. stop *stopping*       shop ..........
   sit *sitting*         run ..........
   get ..........         begin ..........

4. lie *lying*           die ..........

**3** Say these words after the recording or after your teacher.

1. egg    end    send    west
2. he    we        east    eat        meet    sleep

**1 or 2? Decide how to pronounce these words and check with your teacher or the recording.**

| went | meat | men | bed | be | left |
| reading | sheep | mean | me | get | speak |

**Which group do these words go in?**

| many | friend | head | any |

75

# C Things are changing

**1** What is happening to food prices in Fantasia?
Look at the graph and make sentences.

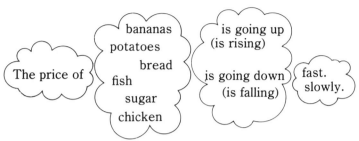

**FOOD PRICES IN FANTASIA**

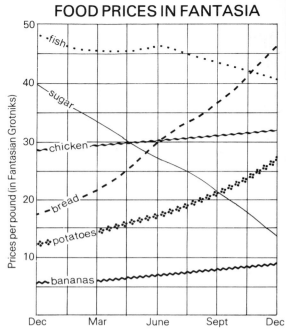

**2** What is happening to prices in your country?

**3** Listen to the figures and complete the table.

| FANTASIA: SOME STATISTICS | 100 YEARS AGO | 50 YEARS AGO | NOW |
|---|---|---|---|
| Population | 20m | 35m | 46m |
| Average number of children per family | 4.5 | 3.6 | 2 |
| Average July temperature | 33°C | ........ | ........ |
| Average January temperature | ........ | ........ | 7°C |
| Average height (men) | ........ | 1m67 | ........ |
| Average height (women) | ........ | 1m62 | ........ |
| Length of working week | 54hrs | ........ | ........ |
| Paid holiday | – | ........ | ........ |
| Average time taken for letter to travel 100km | ........ | 2 days | ........ |
| Size of Fantasian army | 500,000 | ........ | ........ |
| Population of San Fantastico | ........ | ........ | 3m |
| Percentage of population without homes | ........ | ........ | 8% |
| Percentage of population unemployed | ........ | 7% | ........ |

**4** How are things changing in Fantasia? Look at the table and make sentences.

The population    The army    Holidays    The post
The housing problem    People    The climate
The working week    The unemployment problem
The population of San Fantastico    Families

is getting
are getting

bigger/smaller    faster/slower
longer/shorter    taller/shorter
warmer/colder    better/worse

**5** How are things changing in your country?

**Grammar: the two present tenses**

| PRESENT PROGRESSIVE TENSE | SIMPLE PRESENT TENSE |
|---|---|
| I'm working.   You're working.   etc.<br>Am I working?   Are you working?   etc.<br>I'm not working.   You aren't working.   etc. | I work.   You work.   He/she works.   etc.<br>Do I work? Do you work? Does he/she work? etc.<br>I/you don't work.   He/she doesn't work.   etc. |

**We use the Present Progressive tense to talk about:**
1. things that are happening now, these days.
2. things that are changing.

**Examples:**

'Are you free now?' 'Sorry, I'**m studying**.'
'Look. Helen'**s wearing** a lovely dress.'
'What **are** you **cooking**?' 'Steak.'
'My car **isn't going** very well. I must take it to the garage.'
'Food prices **are going up**.'

**We use the Simple Present tense to talk about:**
1. things that are always true.
2. things that happen often, usually, always, never, etc.

**Examples:**

'I always **study** from five to seven o'clock.'
'Helen often **wears** red.'
'I usually **cook** steak for dinner on Saturday.'
'It's a good car. It **doesn't** often **break down**.'

'Food prices **go up** every year.'

**1** Put in the correct verb tense.

1. 'Can you help me for a minute?' 'I'm sorry, .............' (I work / I'm working)
2. ........... on Saturdays? (Do you work / Are you working)
3. 'Have you got a light?' 'Sorry, .............' (I don't smoke / I'm not smoking)
4. How many languages ...........? (do you speak / are you speaking)
5. Why ........... a sweater? It isn't cold. (do you wear / are you wearing)
6. My father ........... to Ireland in August. (always goes / is always going)
7. Robert ........... football most weekends. (plays / is playing)
8. 'Where's Lucy?' '.............' (She shops / She's shopping)
9. 'What ...........?' 'Chocolate.' (do you eat / are you eating)

**2** Listen to the recording and answer the questions.

**3** What are they doing? Listen to the conversation and circle any of these verbs that you hear.

sending   spending   standing   staying
playing   having   working   watching
washing   doing   reading   eating   writing
raining   cleaning   drinking   thinking
looking   cooking   going   opening

**4** Who is doing what? Listen again and fill in the table.

| JANE | is talking to Polly |
|---|---|
| POLLY | |
| JANE'S MOTHER | |
| BILL | |
| THE BABY | |
| SUE | |
| FRANK | |

**5** Look over the summary on page 149 with your teacher.

# Plans

## A  Who's doing what when?

**1** **Read the problem and complete the solution.**

PROBLEM

Arsenal, Manchester, Liverpool and Tottenham are
   four football teams.

Each team is playing against one of the others on
   the next three Saturdays – a different one each
   time.

On Saturday the 12th, Arsenal are playing against
   Manchester.

Manchester are playing against Tottenham on the
   19th.

Who is playing against who on the 26th?

SOLUTION

> Manchester ............ against Arsenal on the 12th,
> ............ they are playing ............ Tottenham on
> the ............ .
>
> ............ on the 26th they ............ against Arsenal
> ............ Tottenham.
>
> ............ they are playing against ............ on the
> 26th.
>
> ............ ............ are playing against ............ on
> the 26th.

**Words to put in:**

> Arsenal    Liverpool    Tottenham    are playing
> are not playing    against    19th    and    or
> so    so    so

After you have solved the problem, you can
listen to a recording of some British people
trying to do it.

**2** **Can you think of some things that are
happening in this town or country during the
next week or so? (Concerts, football matches,
visits, ...)**

**3** **What are you doing this evening? What are
you doing next weekend? What are you doing
for your next holiday?**

**4** **Complete this dialogue and practise it in pairs**

A: Are you doing anything this evening?
B: I'm not sure. Why?
A: Well, would you like to ............ with me?
B: I'd love to, but I'm probably ............ing.
A: Well, how about tomorrow? Are you free?
B: ..................................... .
A: ..................................... .

**5** **Say these words after the recording or after
your teacher.**

1. hungry    husband    industrial    up
2. blue    Tuesday    excuse    rude
3. purple    return    surname    Thursday

**1, 2 or 3? Decide how to pronounce these words
and check with your teacher or the recording.**

> furniture    lunch    supermarket    supper
> true    number    uncle    turn
> June    curly    summer    sun

# B   We're leaving on Monday

(Janet and Bill are talking on Monday April 19th, at nine o'clock in the morning.)

JANET: Is everything all right?
BILL:   Yes, I think so. I'm picking up the visas on Wednesday morning and the tickets in the afternoon, and I'm getting the traveller's cheques from the bank tomorrow.
JANET: Oh, good. Don't forget that the children are going to Mother on the 22nd – you're driving them.
BILL:   Oh, yes. How long for?
JANET: Just for two days. Back on Friday night.
BILL:   That isn't long.
JANET: Darling – you know it's John's birthday on the 24th.
BILL:   So it is. We must have him home for his birthday. What are we giving him?
JANET: A bike.
BILL:   Oh yes, that's right. When are you going to do the packing?
JANET: At the weekend, at the last possible moment. You're going to help, I hope.

BILL:   Oh, yes. Yes, of course.
JANET: And then on Monday we're off! British Airways Flight 011 to Australia. For three months! I'm so excited!
BILL:   OK. Remember Peter and Sally are coming this evening.
JANET: No, they aren't. It's tomorrow.
BILL:   Well, somebody's coming this evening.
JANET: Your father. And Mary Rawson's telephoning this afternoon. She wants to ask you about insurance.
BILL:   Well, I'm sorry, but I'm leaving in about two minutes. I have to be at the office in half an hour, and I won't be back before six.
JANET: All right. I'll give Mary your love.
BILL:   OK. Bye, darling. Have a nice day.
JANET: You too. Bye-bye.

## 1 Put these events in the right order as fast as you can.

A  Bill's visit to the bank
B  John's birthday
C  Mary Rawson's phone call
D  Bill picking up the tickets
E  children leaving to stay with their grandmother
F  family leaving for Australia
G  Bill picking up the visas
H  Peter and Sally's visit
I   Bill leaving for the office
J   Janet packing (with Bill's help)
K  Bill coming back from the office
L  Bill's father's visit

## 2 Janet and Bill are talking at nine o'clock on Monday April 19th. They can talk about the future in two or three different ways. Example:

*on the 22nd = on Thursday = in three days.*

**How could Bill and Janet say these differently?**
*on Wednesday   on the 24th   in a week
at ten o'clock   in three hours   in four days*

## 3 How soon are the following: your birthday; Christmas; the end of your English course; the end of this lesson? (Use *in*.)

## 4 Put *at, on, in, for* or no preposition.

1. What are you doing ........... the weekend?
2. I'm seeing Carlo ........... Tuesday.
3. My mother's telephoning ........... three o'clock.
4. 'Can I talk to you?' 'Sorry, I'm leaving ........... five minutes.'
5. I think it's going to rain ........... this afternoon.
6. We're going to Dakar in June ........... three weeks.
7. Would you like to go out with me ........... Monday evening?
8. Telephone me ........... tomorrow if you have time.
9. 'I'm going to Norway ........... August.' 'That's nice. How long ...........?'

## 5 Are you going on a journey soon? If so, tell the class about it.

# C  Let's go to Scotland

**1** How far do you think these places are from each other? (The distances are in the table.)

I think Oxford is ............ from London.
I think Moscow is ............ from Paris.
I think San Francisco is ............ from Miami.
I think London is ............ from Edinburgh.
I think Paris is ............ from London.
I think Peking is ............ from Caracas.

| MILES | 60 | 209 | 378 | 1540 | 2582 | 10350 |
|---|---|---|---|---|---|---|
| KILOMETRES | 96 | 336 | 608 | 2478 | 4155 | 16656 |

Listen to a recording of some English-speaking people trying to answer the questions.

**2** Suggestions.

Listen to the conversations.
There are three answers to the first suggestion.
What are they?
What are the three answers to the second
  suggestion?

| SUGGESTION | ANSWERS |
|---|---|
| Let's go to Scotland for our holiday. | 1. ................................. |
| | 2. ................................. |
| | 3. ................................. |

| SUGGESTION | ANSWERS |
|---|---|
| Why don't we go to California? | 1. ................................. |
| | 2. ................................. |
| | 3. ................................. |

*"Somewhere with no
irregular verbs."*

**3** Work in groups of four. Prepare and practise conversations about holidays, films, restaurants, visits, or evening/weekend activities. One student makes a suggestion; the others answer. Examples of suggestions:

*'Let's go to ............ for our holiday.'*
*'Let's go and see (name of film).'*
*'Let's have lunch/dinner at (name of restaurant).'*
*'Let's go and see (name of friend).'*
*'Let's go and see a film this evening.'*
*'Let's go to Scotland this weekend.'*

**4** Listen to the recording. How many words are there? What are they? (Contractions like *don't* count as two words.)

*"Artie, how would you pack if you were going to Mars?"*

# D Meet me at eight

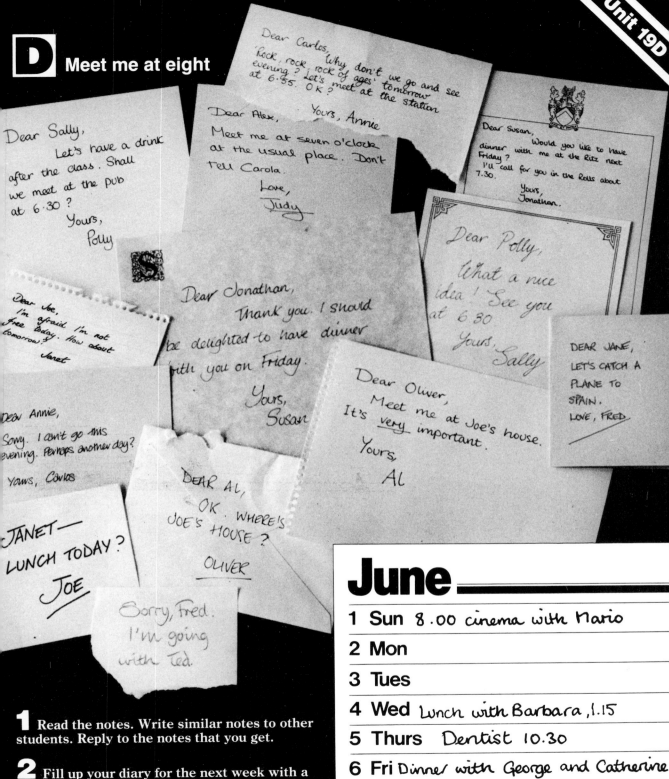

Dear Carlos,
Why don't we go and see 'Rock, rock, rock of ages' tomorrow evening? Let's meet at the station at 6.55. OK?

Yours, Annie

Dear Sally,
Let's have a drink after the class. Shall we meet at the pub at 6.30?

Yours, Polly

Dear Alex,
Meet me at seven o'clock at the usual place. Don't tell Carola.

Love, Judy

Dear Susan,
Would you like to have dinner with me at the Ritz next Friday? I'll call for you in the Rolls about 7.30.

Yours, Jonathan.

Dear Joe,
I'm afraid I'm not free today. How about tomorrow?

Janet

Dear Jonathan,
Thank you. I should be delighted to have dinner with you on Friday.

Yours, Susan

Dear Polly,
What a nice idea! See you at 6.30

Yours, Sally

DEAR JANE,
LET'S CATCH A PLANE TO SPAIN.
LOVE, FRED

Dear Annie,
Sorry. I can't go this evening. Perhaps another day?

Yours, Carlos

Dear Oliver,
Meet me at Joe's house. It's very important.

Yours, Al

JANET—
LUNCH TODAY?
JOE

DEAR AL,
OK. WHERE'S JOE'S HOUSE?

OLIVER

Sorry, Fred.
I'm going with Ted.

**1** Read the notes. Write similar notes to other students. Reply to the notes that you get.

**2** Fill up your diary for the next week with a list of appointments.

**3** Look at the summary on page 149 with your teacher.

# June

| 1 Sun | 8.00 cinema with Mario |
| 2 Mon | |
| 3 Tues | |
| 4 Wed | Lunch with Barbara, 1.15 |
| 5 Thurs | Dentist 10.30 |
| 6 Fri | Dinner with George and Catherine |
| 7 Sat | Henry's Party. |
| 8 Sun | |
| 9 Mon | Meeting with M.C. |

# Getting to know you

## A Is this seat free?

**1** Look at the pictures. What do you think the people are saying in each picture?

**2** Revision. Ask to borrow things from other students.

'Could I borrow your pen?'
'Yes, of course.'

'Can I use your dictionary for a moment?'
'Yes, here you are.'

'Can I borrow your watch?'
'Sorry, I need it.'

**3** Work with another student. You are on a train, and you want to sit down, open the window, etc. Ask and answer.

| ASK FOR PERMISSION | GIVE PERMISSION |
|---|---|
| Do you mind if I sit here? | Not at all. |
| Do you mind if I open the window? | No, please do. |
| | Go ahead. |
| Do you mind if I smoke? | REFUSE PERMISSION |
| Do you mind if I look at your paper? | I'm sorry. It's not free. |
| | Well, it's a bit cold. |
| | Well, I'd rather you didn't. |
| | Well, I'm reading it myself, actually. |

**4** Close your books, listen to the recording and answer.

a. Give permission.
b. Refuse permission.

**5** Improvisation.
Work in groups of between four and six. You are sitting together on a train. Begin a conversation.
OR:
Work in pairs. You are both in a coffee-bar, a pub or a park. Begin a conversation.

**6** Pronunciation. Say these words and expressions.

a. Is this seat free?
b. seat  sit  eat  it  sheep  ship
c. heat  need  cheap
   steam  steel  leak
   seek  peach  keep
d. win  spit  hit  pick  lip

# B Do you often come here?

I always come here on
Sunday mornings.
Oh, do you? So do I...

Do you like 'Top of the Pops'?
I never watch it...

My brother...
Does he?...

I'm Pisces.
Are you? So am I...

I go to the cinema at least once a week...
*How often do you...?*
Every two or three days...

I've got a...
*Oh, have you?...*

*Do you ever go to the opera?* Oh, yes. I love opera.
*So do I. Actually, I've got two tickets for*
*'Carmen' tonight.* Oh, have you?
*Would you like to go with me?*
I'd love to.
*Let's go and have a drink.*
Why not?

## 1 Ask and answer.

How often do you:

go to the hairdresser / watch TV / travel by
train / go on holiday / go for a walk / go to
the cinema / listen to records / go skiing /
write letters / drink beer / drink coffee /
eat in a restaurant / go swimming / go
dancing / play tennis / wash your hair?

Very often.  Sometimes.  Hardly ever.
Quite often.  Occasionally.  Never.

Once
Twice
Three times
a day.
a week.
a month.
a year.

Every day/week/month/Tuesday.
Every three days/six weeks.

## 2 Word order. Write sentences like the examples.

*I never go to the
cinema
I often listen to records.*

*I go skiing twice a year.
I travel by train every
Tuesday.*

## 3 Reply questions. Match sentences and answers. Practise the intonation. Then close your books and answer the recorded sentences.

| | |
|---|---|
| My brother's a doctor. | Do you?   Oh, yes? |
| My sister's got five children. | Is it?   Really? |
| Maria likes fast cars. | Is he? |
| It's raining again. | Has she? |
| I slept badly last night. | Are you? |
| I love skiing. | Can he? |
| My father can speak five languages. | Does she? |
| I'm tired. | Did you? |

## 4 Work in pairs. Tell your partner things about yourself, your friends and your family. Your partner will answer 'Are you?' 'Do you?' etc.

# C What do you think of...?

**1** Read the picture story. Your teacher will help you.

**2** Look at the questions in frame 3. Choose possible answers from these.

> Yes, I do.    For about seven years.    Terrible!
> Cheesecake.    No, I don't.    Yes, lots of times.
> All my life.    Not bad.    No, I haven't.    Great!
> Not much.    No, never.

**3** Ask other students questions about well-known singers, writers, etc.

> She's not bad.

> She's very good.

> What do you think of...?

> I like her.

> Terrible!

**4** What are their favourite colours? Listen to the recording to find out.

> red    orange    yellow    green    blue
> purple    light blue    light green

Now ask other students *What's/Who's your favourite...?*
Then copy the form and fill it in.

> MY FAVOURITE FOOD .....................
> MY FAVOURITE COLOUR .....................
> MY FAVOURITE GAME/SPORT .....................
> MY FAVOURITE WRITER .....................
> MY FAVOURITE SINGER .....................
> MY FAVOURITE PLACE .....................
> MY FAVOURITE SEASON .....................
> MY FAVOURITE ANIMAL .....................

**5** Match the sentences and the answers. (Two answers for each sentence.)

> I like fish.    I'm tired.
> I've got too much work.
> I can speak German.

> So can I.    I haven't.    I don't.    So am I.
> So have I.    I can't.    I'm not.    So do I.

**6** Say things about yourself beginning:
*I like ...   I'm ...   I've got ...   I can ...*
The class will answer: *So do I, I don't,* etc.

**7** Pronunciation. Say these words.

who    how    hundred    have    half    hair
hand    hate    house    hello

# D  I've only known her for twenty-four hours, but...

*the nicest*

I've met for years. I've only
since yesterday, but I'm already
it's going to be very important
tall and slim, with a beautif
and - believe it or not, Sally—
interested in the same things as
films, music, travel and so on.
Pisces, and so

*met this wonderf*
John, I really think I'
It's funny. I've only
for 24 hours, but I feel
each other all our lives.
so many interests in common:
films, travel... We're bot

**1** Can you complete the sentences in the two torn letters? These words and expressions will help.

| We've got | music |
|---|---|
| Pisces. | known her |
| girl. | we've known |
| in love | |

| sure | he's | He's |
|---|---|---|
| I am: | man | |
| known him | | am I. |
| smile | He's | |

**2** How long have you lived in your city/town/village/etc.? Examples:

'I've lived in Cardiff since 1979.'
'I've lived in Boston for the last five years.'
'I've lived in London all my life.'

**3** *Since* and *for.*

since yesterday = for 24 hours
since the 16th century = for 400 years
since last Tuesday = for ............
since last ............ = for five days
since 1977 = for ............
............ = since my birthday
since nine o'clock = ............
since last July = ............
for ten years = ............

**4** Ask and answer (with *since* or *for*).

| 'How long have you | been in this town?' |
|---|---|
| | been in this class?' |
| | been learning English?' |
| | been married?' |
| | etc. |

| 'How long have you had | that watch?' |
|---|---|
| | that sweater?' |
| | that ring?' |
| | etc. |

| 'How long have you known | the teacher?' |
|---|---|
| | your friend Alex?' |
| | etc. |

**5** Ask and answer.

| 'Have you (ever) read...?' | 'Yes, I have.' | 'What did you **think** of it?' | 'Great.' |
|---|---|---|---|
| 'Have you (ever) seen...?' | 'No, I haven't.' | | 'Not bad.' |
| 'Have you (ever) been to...?' | 'Not yet.' | | 'OK.' |
| | | | 'I didn't like it.' |
| | | | etc. |

**6** Look at the summary on page 150 with your teacher.

# Things

## A  Why...? Because...

**1** Listen to the song; find out what the words mean.

### WHY, OH WHY?

Why can't a dish break a hammer?
Tell me why, oh why?
Because a hammer's
got a pretty hard head.
Goodbye, goodbye, goodbye.

Why can't a bird eat an elephant?
Tell me why, oh why?
Well, for one thing an
elephant's got a very
tough skin.
Goodbye, goodbye, goodbye.

Why, oh why, oh why, oh why
Tell me why, oh why?
Just because, because, because, because.
Goodbye, goodbye.

Now why won't you answer my question?
Tell me why, oh why?
Because to tell you the plain truth, honey,
I just don't know the answers.

Goodbye, goodbye.

(*Why, oh Why* by Woody Guthrie © copyright 1960, 1964, and 1972 Ludlow Music, Inc.)

**2** Answer these questions; use *too*. You can use a dictionary.
Example: WHY CAN'T YOU PICK UP A CAR? BECAUSE IT'S TOO HEAVY.

**You can use these words in the answers:**

| | | | | | |
|---|---|---|---|---|---|
| heavy | cold | light | big | quiet | soft |
| hard | strong | tall | loud | dark | hot |
| wide | high | small | | | |

1. Why can't a knife cut a stone?
2. Why can't you jump over a house?
3. Why can't you throw a fridge?
4. Why can't you sunbathe at the North Pole?
5. Why can't you put a car in your bath?
6. Why can't you hear your heart beating?
7. Why can't you drink boiling water?
8. Why can't you read in a forest in the middle of the night?
9. Why can't you jump across the Mississippi?
10. Why can't you eat rice before it's cooked?
11. Why can't you stand up in a car?

**3** Now answer the same questions again; use *enough*.
Example: WHY CAN'T YOU PICK UP A CAR? BECAUSE I'M NOT STRONG ENOUGH.

**4** Match the opposites.

| | | | | | | | | | |
|---|---|---|---|---|---|---|---|---|---|
| heavy | light | wide | big | quiet | tall | hard | cold | high | loud |
| small | hot | light | short | quiet | low | dark | narrow | soft | noisy |

**5** Look round the classroom, and try to find something heavy, something light, something wide, something narrow, etc. Use the adjectives from Exercise 4.

**6** Which one is different? Why?

1. a tent    the Empire State Building    the Eiffel Tower    St Paul's Cathedral
2. Siberia    Greenland    Morocco    Alaska
3. a flower    a leaf    a gold watch    a hair
4. Russia    Wales    China    South America
5. butter    wool    a knife    a mushroom

# B  What's a car made of?

**1** Use your dictionary. Look at the pictures and find out what the different things are made of.
**Example:** *'The fifth object is made of leather.'*

**2** What are these made of?

a clock    a car    a cinema
a sofa    a TV    a secretary's chair
**Example:** *'A cinema is made of metal, stone, ...'*

**3** Listen. Which three objects are the people talking about? Number them 1, 2, 3.

a car    an armchair    a typewriter
a bicycle    a coat    a fridge

**4** Animal, vegetable, mineral or abstract?

a glass    a woollen sweater    a book
a pair of shoes    a typewriter    a tree
a cassette    an idea    age    your nose

**5** Twenty questions. Think of an object.

Tell the other students whether it is animal, vegetable, mineral or abstract. They must find out what it is; they can ask twenty questions, but you can only answer *'Yes'* or *'No'*.
**Possible questions:**

*'Can you eat it?'*
*'Is it made of wood/metal/glass/...?'*
*'Is it useful?'*
*'Can you find it in a house/shop/car/...?'*
*'Is it liquid?'*
*'Is it hard/soft/heavy/light/...?'*
*'Have you got one of these?'*
*'Is it manufactured?'*
*'Is there one in this room?'*

**Then listen to some people playing 'Twenty questions.'**

# C 'The best car in the world'

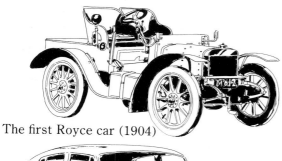

The first Royce car (1904)

The Silver Ghost (1906-1925)

The Silver Cloud
(1959-1966)

The Silver Spirit (1981)

Henry Royce did not like his Decauville car, which ran badly and often broke down. So he decided to make a better car himself, and in 1904 he produced his first two-cylinder model. Charles Rolls, a car manufacturer, was very impressed by Royce's car, and soon Rolls and Royce went into business together. One of their first models was the Silver Ghost. In 1907, a Silver Ghost broke the world's endurance record by driving 14,371 miles (23,120km) without breaking down once. After the drive, it cost just over £2 to put the car back into perfect condition. It is not surprising that the Silver Ghost was called 'the best car in the world'. Rolls-Royce cars are famous for running quietly: an advertisement for one model said 'the loudest noise is the ticking of the clock'. The cars are made very carefully. A lot of the work is done by hand, and they take a long time to manufacture: only twelve cars leave the factory every day.

## 1 What do you think these words and expressions mean?
Look at the text, but do not use a dictionary.
Choose one answer for each question.

1. *It broke down*:     a. It made a noise.
   b. Pieces fell off it.     c. It stopped working.
2. *Charles Rolls was very impressed by Royce's car*:
   a. He thought it was good.     b. He wanted it.
   c. He did not understand it.
3. *model*:     a. picture     b. small car
   c. sort of car
4. *endurance*:     a. going fast     b. going on for a long time     c. being easy to drive
5. *Rolls-Royce cars are famous*:     a. They are very good.     b. Everybody knows about them.
   c. They are very quiet.
6. *ticking*:     a. a sort of clock     b. a part of a car
   c. a sort of noise
7. *manufacture*:     a. make     b. sell     c. finish
8. *factory*:     a. town     b. place where cars are made     c. shop

## 2 Choose an object from the list in the box. Ask other students these questions about it. Note their answers and report to the class.

| car    motorbike    watch    radio |
| cassette player    television    calculator |
| camera |

1. Have you got a ............?
2. How long have you had it?
3. Where was it made?
4. Where did you buy it?
5. Has it ever broken down?
6. Have you used it a lot?
7. Are you happy with it, or would you like a better one?

# D Where was your car made?

## 1 Where are they made?

**Example:** *'Wine is made in Italy, France, . . .'*

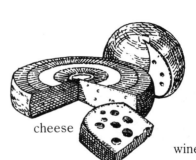

cheese

wine

perfume

cameras

cars

shoes

calculators

## 2 Ask other students, and answer.

*'Where was your car made?' 'Where were your shoes made?'* etc.

## 3 Exports. Japan exports cameras to Britain. France exports wine to the USA. Help your teacher add more examples to the table.

| PRODUCER | PRODUCT | CUSTOMER |
|----------|---------|----------|
| Japan | cameras | Britain |
| France | wine | the USA |
| . . . | . . . | . . . |

## 4 Imports. What does your country import, and where from? Copy the table, fill it up with examples, and tell another student about it.

| NAME OF COUNTRY | |
|-----------------|--|
| PRODUCT | PRODUCER |
| | |

## 5 Say these sentences.

1. Germany exports cars. Italy exports wine. The USA exports corn. Turkey imports radios.
2. Mexico exports oil. Morocco exports oranges.
3. Canada exports paper. India imports chemicals.

## 6 Read the text. Use a dictionary or ask your teacher for help.

### SOME OF BRITAIN'S IMPORTS AND EXPORTS

Britain imports petroleum, mainly from the Middle East and Libya; cars from Europe and Japan; lamb and butter from New Zealand; and fruit from the EEC, South America and Africa.

Some of Britain's exports are: chemicals, which are produced all over the country; chocolate and sugar confectionery, which are made mostly in York and the South West; drinks, which are produced mainly in Scotland; and metals and metal products, which are manufactured in many regions including Yorkshire, South Wales, the Midlands and the Northern Region.

## 7 Fill in the blanks with words from the text in Exercise 6.

### SOME OF AUSTRALIA'S IMPORTS AND EXPORTS

Australia ............ books from Britain, electronic equipment ............ Japan, ............ cars and heavy machines ............ Britain and the USA. Some of Australia's exports are: wool, ............ is produced ............ in the dry regions and ............ New South Wales; wheat, which ............ grown in ............ south-east and in the region of Perth; sugar, which is ............ mainly in Queensland; and minerals (lead, zinc, etc.), which ............ imported ............ by Britain and Japan.

## 8 Write a text about some of your country's exports and imports.

## 9 Read through the summary on page 152 with your teacher.

# Revision and fluency practice

## A Comparison

Dürer - Self-portrait

Clouet - Francois I,
King of France

**1** **How many differences can you find between the two pictures? Examples:**

*'Dürer's hair is lighter than the king's.'*
*'Dürer's hands are together; the king's are not.'*

**2** **Listen, and choose the correct one. Example:**

*1. 'It's smaller than a piano; it's got more strings than a violin.'* **Answer:** *'Guitar.'*

1. piano    clarinet    organ    guitar    violin
2. cloud    snow    sun    ice    rain
3. dog    mouse    kangaroo    cat    elephant
4. fridge    car    cooker    typewriter    bus
5. horse    taxi    bicycle    car    bus
6. Everest    Mont Blanc    Eiffel Tower    tree
7. Japan    Kenya    France    Germany    Norway
8. champagne    whisky    Coca Cola    milk
9. wool    wood    iron    glass    aluminium

**3** **Now make your own questions about these.**

1. sofa    chair    table    wardrobe    TV
2. shirt    raincoat    skirt    shoe    belt
3. India    Tibet    Bolivia    Switzerland    Canada
4. The USA    The USSR    China    Norway    Ghana
5. London    Paris    New York    Hong Kong    Cairo
6. elephant    whale    double-decker bus    bicycle    cat
7. doctor    teacher    dentist    shop assistant    footballer
8. cheese    carrot    potato    ice-cream    apple

# B  Sketches

**1** Work in groups of three or four.
Some of you are shop assistants:

and some of you want to buy things:

Prepare and practise a sketch. Use all the English you can.

**2** Getting to know somebody. Work in groups. Prepare and practise a sketch with several characters, using the new language from Unit 20 and some of the other words and expressions that you have learnt. Include some of the following:

| | | | |
| --- | --- | --- | --- |
| getting to know somebody | asking for things | lending and borrowing | exchanging opinions |
| saying how often you do things | telling the time | names | addresses | telephone numbers |
| spelling | telephoning | complimenting | asking the way | a meal in a restaurant | a letter | offering |

# C People

**1** Prepare a copy of the form. Work with a student that you don't know very well.
Ask him/her questions about him/herself, and fill in the answers.

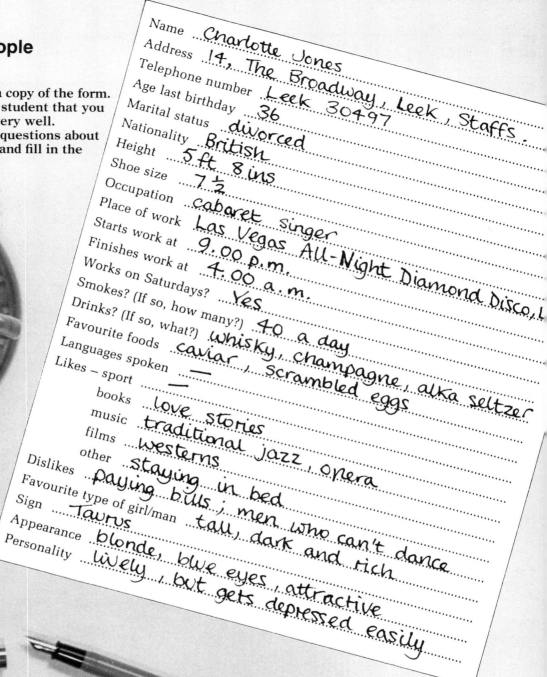

Name ... Charlotte Jones
Address ... 14, The Broadway, Leek, Staffs.
Telephone number ... Leek 30497
Age last birthday ... 36
Marital status ... divorced
Nationality ... British
Height ... 5 ft. 8 ins
Shoe size ... 7½
Occupation ... cabaret singer
Place of work ... Las Vegas All-Night Diamond Disco, L
Starts work at ... 9.00 p.m.
Finishes work at ... 4.00 a.m.
Works on Saturdays? ... Yes
Smokes? (If so, how many?) ... 40 a day
Drinks? (If so, what?) ... whisky, champagne, alka seltzer
Favourite foods ... caviar, scrambled eggs
Languages spoken ... —
Likes – sport ... —
        books ... love stories
        music ... traditional jazz, opera
        films ... westerns
        other ... staying in bed
Dislikes ... paying bills; men who can't dance
Favourite type of girl/man ... tall, dark and rich
Sign ... Taurus
Appearance ... blonde, blue eyes, attractive
Personality ... lively, but gets depressed easily

**2** Find five things that you have in common with the student you interviewed, and five differences. Say what they are. Examples:

*'He drinks Coke, and so do I.'*
*'He is tall, and so am I.'*
*'He likes driving fast cars, but I don't.'*
*'He's got blue eyes, but I haven't.'*

**3** Work in pairs. One student's mother/father/ grandmother/grandfather/aunt/uncle/child/ friend has disappeared; the other student is a policeman or policewoman. The first student gives a detailed description of the missing person; the other asks questions.

# D Listening and grammar

**1** Listen to the recording and fill in the table.

| | DEPARTURE TIME | DESTINATION | ARRIVAL TIME | CHANGE? |
|---|---|---|---|---|
| 1 | | | | |
| 2 | | | | |
| 3 | | | | |
| 4 | | | | |
| 5 | | | | |

**Place names:** Hereford Victoria  Ashton  Stoke Adderbury  Caldon London  Reading Birmingham  Manchester Ashford

**2** Listen to the sounds. What is happening? Example:

*1. Somebody is walking.*

**3** Complete the sentences.

1. Look! It ............ (rains / is raining)
2. It always ........... on Sundays. (rains / is raining)
3. 'What ...........?' 'I'm looking at the weather forecast.' (do you do / are you doing)
4. '........... oysters?' 'Yes, I love them.' (Do you like / Are you liking)
5. 'Have you got a cigarette?' 'Sorry, I ............' (don't smoke / am not smoking)
6. 'What time ...........?' 'At seven o'clock, usually.' (do you get up / are you getting up)
7. 'Can you come and see me tomorrow?' 'Sorry. ............' (I work / I'm working)
8. I ........... on Saturdays. (usually work / am usually working)
9. 'Is John here?' 'No, ........... football.' (he plays / he's playing)

**4** Put in the right tense: Simple Past, Present Perfect or Present.

1. 'I ........... John yesterday.' (saw / have seen)
2. 'Did you? I ........... him for weeks.' (didn't see / haven't seen)
3. How long ........... living here? (are you / have you been)
4. I ........... Mary since 1980. (know / have known)
5. I think I ........... her very well. (know / have known)
6. ........... to India? (Have you ever been / Did you ever go)
7. ........... his latest book? (Have you read / Did you read)
8. How long ........... that watch? (have you had / did you have / do you have)

**5** Put in *since*, *for* or *ago*.

1. We've lived in London ........... eight years.
2. I've only known her ........... yesterday.
3. My grandmother died three years ............
4. I've been working ........... four o'clock this morning.
5. She's been a teacher ........... eighteen years.
6. It's been raining ........... three days.
7. I first went to Africa about seven years ............
8. Mary phoned a few minutes ............
9. I haven't seen her ........... weeks.

93

# Instructions

## A How to do it

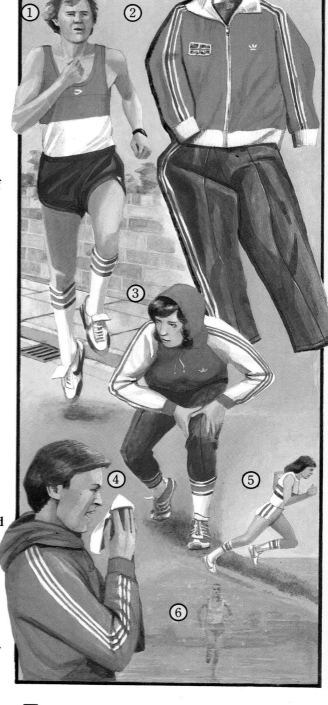

**1** Here is some advice about running. Some of it is good, and some is not. Which sentences give you good advice?

RUNNING① – DOs and DON'Ts

Wear good running shoes.
Run early in the morning – it's better.
Wear comfortable clothing②.
Always warm up③ before you run.
Always run with somebody – never run alone.
Rest every ten minutes or so.
Walk for a few minutes after you finish.

Don't run if you feel tired.
Never drink water while you are running.
Don't run until two hours after eating.
Don't run if you have got a cold④.
Don't run fast downhill⑤.
Don't run if you are over 50.
Don't run on roads in fog⑥.

**When you have finished the exercise, listen to some British people trying to do it.**

**2** Work in groups. Think of some advice (good or bad) for one of the following.

– a tourist in your country
– somebody who is learning to drive
– somebody who is learning your language
– somebody who is learning English
– somebody who wants to get rich
– somebody who wants more friends

**Make a list of three (or more) DOs and three (or more) DON'Ts.**

**3** Listen, and try to draw the picture.

**4** Work in groups.
One student draws a simple picture, but does not show it to the others.
He or she gives the others instructions, and they try to draw the same picture.

**5** Say these words after the recording or your teacher.

1. fog    hot    long    doctor    dollar    office
2. comfortable    front    another    brother

**Find some more words that go in group 1.
Can you find any more that go in group 2?**

94

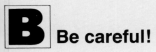

# B Be careful!

**1** Put the following expressions into the pictures.

> Please hurry!   Take your time.   Don't worry.   Look.   Come in.   Wait here, please.
> Be careful.   Follow me, please.   Look out!

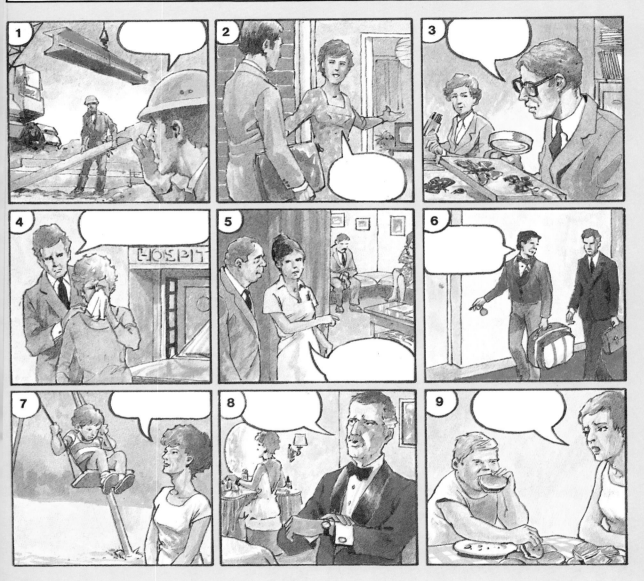

**2** Work in groups. Prepare and practise a very short sketch using one or more of the expressions from Exercise 1.

**3** Listen to the recording.
Write ✓ every time you hear an imperative (like *Walk, Come in, Be careful*), and ✗ every time you hear a negative imperative (like *Don't run, Don't worry*).
Listen again, and then try to remember some of the imperatives and negative imperatives.

# C On and off

**1** Look at the picture. Where are things? Where should they be? Example:

*'There's a chair on the piano. It should be on the floor.'*

| Useful words: | on | in | under | by |
|---|---|---|---|---|

**2** Some friends are going to help you to put things in the right places.
**What will you say to them? Example:**

*'Could you take the chair off the piano and put it by the window?'*

| Useful words: | take | put | off | out of | in(to) |
|---|---|---|---|---|---|

**3** Listen to the song and try to put in the missing words. Your teacher will help you with vocabulary.

'I dropped my ............'
'Pick ............ up, pick ............ up
and put ............ away in ............ closet.'

'I dropped my ............'
'Pick ............ up, pick ............ up
and throw ............ away ............ basket.'

'I dropped my ............'
'Pick ............ up, pick ............ up
and wash ............ clean in the ............,'

'I dropped my dolly.'
'Pick ............ up, pick ............ up
and ............ back in ............ cradle.'

'I dropped my toys.'
'Pick ............ up, pick ............ up
and put ............ back in ............ places.'

(*Pick it up* by Woody Guthrie; © copyright 1954
Folkways Music Publishers, Inc.)

# D Recipes

# Mushroom Salad

**Ingredients**
½ lb white mushrooms, very fresh
1 tablespoon lemon juice
Pepper, salt
A few chives or a little parsley
4 tablespoons olive oil

**Utensils**
Bowl   Fork
Clean cloth   Knife

**Time**
10 mins to prepare,
1½ hrs to stand.

1. Wash mushrooms and pat dry. (Do not peel.) Cut off most of stalk. Slice the rest thinly and put in salad bowl.
2. Mix oil with lemon juice, salt and pepper, and beat well.
3. Pour about ⅔ of this dressing over mushrooms, stir gently and put aside for an hour.
4. Add rest of dressing and put aside again until most of dressing is absorbed, about ½ hour.
5. Meanwhile, chop chives or parsley. Sprinkle this over salad, and serve.

(from *The Beginner's Cookery Book* by Betty Falk)

**1** Match each picture to one of the numbered instructions in the recipe. Use one number twice.

A

B

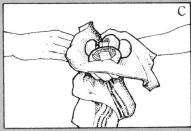
C

D

E

F

**2** Listen to someone telling you how to make a mushroom salad. The grammar of the spoken recipe is different from that of the written recipe. In what ways?

**3** Write a recipe (begin *Ingredients*......).
Then give instructions to another student.
(Begin '*You take...*') Here are some words you can use:
*saucepan, frying-pan, casserole, oven, fry, boil, melt.*

**4** Look at the summary on page 153 with your teacher.

# Getting around

## A  A room for two nights

### 1 Study and practise the dialogue.

RECEPTIONIST: Can I help you?
TRAVELLER:    Yes, I'd like a room, please.
RECEPTIONIST: Single or double?
TRAVELLER:    Single, please.
RECEPTIONIST: For one night?
TRAVELLER:    No, two nights.
RECEPTIONIST: With bath or with shower?
TRAVELLER:    With bath, please. How much is the room?
RECEPTIONIST: £23 a night, including breakfast.
TRAVELLER:    Can I pay by credit card?
RECEPTIONIST: Yes, of course. Could you register, please?
TRAVELLER:    Pardon?
RECEPTIONIST: Could you fill in the form, please?
TRAVELLER:    Oh, yes.
RECEPTIONIST: Your room number is 403. Have a good stay.
TRAVELLER:    Thank you.

### 2 Think of other expressions that can be useful in a hotel. Ask your teacher how to say them.

### 3 Work with a partner. Make up a new traveller–receptionist conversation, with as many changes as possible. Your teacher will help you.

### 4 Answer the questions. Time-limit: five minutes.

1. What street is the Hilton Hotel in?
2. How many cars can be parked in the Hilton garage?
3. How far is the Hilton from Victoria Station?
4. How many other Hilton hotels are there in London?
5. How much do guests at the Hilton pay for children if they sleep in the same room as their parents?

## Hilton International London

### Hotel Features:

- Address: 22 Park Lane, London W1A 2HH, England
- Telephone: 01-493-8000 Telex: 24873 Cable: HILTELS–London
- Located in the heart of Mayfair, overlooking Hyde Park Minutes from the elegant shopping and theatre districts
- 40 minutes from Heathrow Airport, 45 minutes from London–Gatwick Airport, 5 minutes from Victoria Station
- 509 comfortable guest rooms featuring:
  individual climate control
  direct-dial telephone
  electronic locks for maximum security
  radio and taped music
  self service mini-bar
  television with in-house films
- 104 one- two- and three bedroom suites
- 5 restaurants, cocktail lounge, bar and discotheque
- 24-hour room service
- Same day laundry/valet service at no extra charge (Monday-Friday)
- Meeting facilities for up to 1000 persons
- 24-hour telex, cable, interpreter, secretarial service, typewriters, mail and postage facilities
- Pocket bleepers available for individual guest paging
- Worldwide courier service for documents guaranteeing one to three day delivery
- Teleplan – guarantees reasonable surcharges on international telephone calls
- Currency exchange at daily bank rates plus a modest handling charge of approximately 1% to cover only direct expenses
- Guest shops including beauty and barber, fashion, florist, drugstore, newsstand, speciality shops and transportation desk
- Indoor parking for 350 cars
- Hilton International Family Plan: there is no room charge for one or more children, regardless of age, when sharing the same room(s) with their parent(s) Maximum occupancy per room 3 persons

In England, there are two other fine Hilton International hotels – Hilton International Kensington on Holland Park Avenue near London's West End, and Hilton International Stratford-upon-Avon, 5 minutes from the Royal Shakespeare Theatre. And look for the new Gatwick Hilton International.

For reservations call your travel agent, any Hilton hotel or Hilton Reservation Service

# B You have to change twice

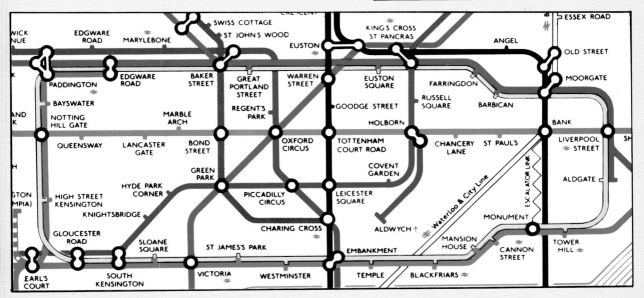

Lines.... VICTORIA  CENTRAL  CIRCLE  DISTRICT  METROPOLITAN  NORTHERN  BAKERLOO  PICCADILLY  JUBILEE

## 1 The London Underground. True or False?

1. Baker St is on the way from Paddington to Euston Square.
2. You can get from Victoria to Baker St without changing.
3. To get from Oxford Circus to Paddington, you have to change twice.
4. Piccadilly Circus is on the way from South Kensington to Bond St.
5. You can get from Bond St to Leicester Square without changing.
6. If you go from Edgware Rd to Hyde Park Corner by the shortest way, you have to change twice.
7. You can go there by a longer way without changing.
8. Notting Hill Gate is on the same line as Holborn.
9. You can't get from Covent Garden to Victoria without changing.
10. If you travel east from Temple on the Circle Line, you can change to the Bakerloo Line at the first stop.
11. If you go from Notting Hill Gate to Green Park, you have to change at the fourth stop.
12. Knightsbridge is not on the way from Paddington to Oxford Circus.

## 2 Make up your own true or false sentences about the London Underground, and test other students with them.

## 3 San Fantastico, the capital of Fantasia, has got a new underground system, with two lines and six stops. Read the sentences and draw a map of the SF Underground.

1. Miller Rd and High St are on the same line.
2. To get from Tower Park to Royce Rd you have to change at the first stop.
3. Tower Park is on the way from Miller Rd to Ship St.
4. If you travel east from High St, Ship St is the first stop.
5. High St is on the same line as Green St.
6. You can go from Royce Rd to Green St without changing.

## 4 Do number 1 or number 2.

1. If all the students in the class are from the same place, make up true or false sentences about the transport system in your own city/country.

2. If the students in the class are from different places, tell the other students two things about the transport system in your city/country.

# C Flight 3 to Hong Kong

## 1 Which picture?

1. Your passport and boarding card, please, sir.
2. British Airways Flight 3 to Hong Kong boarding now at Gate 11.
3. British Airways announce the arrival of Flight 623 from Geneva.
4. I'd like to change my reservation, please.
5. Have you any hand baggage, madam?

## 2 What do these mean? Make sure you know. Then find each one in the timetable.

| British Airways flight number 3 | arrival time | Wednesday | departure time | Monday |
| Boeing 747 Jumbo Jet plane | stopping at | Sunday | minutes | minimum |

## LONDON – HONG KONG 747

DEPART London, Heathrow Airport, Terminal 3 (Minimum check-in time 60 mins; BA First & Club class 45 mins)
ARRIVE Hong Kong, Kai Tak Airport

| Frequency | Aircraft | | Via | Transfer Times | Flight | Air-craft | Class & Catering |
|---|---|---|---|---|---|---|---|
| | Dep | Arr | | | BA3 | 747 | PCM ✗ |
| Mo | 1025 | 0835† | Abu Dhabi | | BA3 | 747 | PCM ✗ |
| Tu | 1700 | 1535† | Bombay | | BA3 | 747 | PCM ✗ |
| We | 1025 | 1035† | Rome, Bahrain | | BA3 | 747 | PCM ✗ |
| Th | 1700 | 1535† | Bombay | | BA3 | 747 | PCM ✗ |
| Fr | 1025 | 0835† | Abu Dhabi | | BA3 | 747 | PCM ✗ |
| Sa | 1700 | 1645† | Rome, Calcutta | | BA3 | 747 | PCM ✗ |
| Su | 1700 | 1520† | Bahrain | | BA3 | 747 | PCM ✗ |

† – Next day

## 3 Answer the questions by looking at the timetable, and make new questions to ask other students.

1. What time does the Hong Kong flight leave London on Tuesdays?
2. What is the flight number?
3. How often does the flight go via Abu Dhabi?
4. What time do flights via Bombay arrive in Hong Kong?
5. On what days can you go from London to Hong Kong via Rome?
6. Where does the flight stop on Wednesdays?
7. By what time must you check in for the Wednesday flight?

## 4 Listen to the announcements and complete the sentences.

1. Passengers for Birmingham on Flight BD ............ – this flight is now boarding at gate number ............ .
2. British Midland passengers to East Midlands on ............ BD ............ – this flight is now boarding at ............ ............ ............ .
3. Would Mr Mattox travelling to ............ please contact the British Airways ............ office opposite island J on the ............ floor?
4. Would Mr Rowley from ............ please ............ British Midland ............?

## 5 Listen to the recording. How many words are there in each sentence? What are they? (Contractions like *don't, I've* count as two words.)

# D  Walk along the river bank...

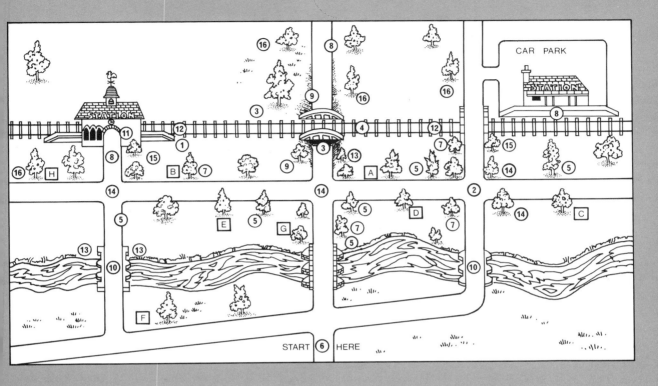

## 1 Treasure hunt. The treasure is buried under one of the trees, at A, B, C, D, E, F, G or H. Follow the clues and find it. Start by reading clue number 6.

1. Go to the nearest railway station. Go into the station.
2. Keep straight on until you see the next clue.
3. Climb up on to the railway line.
4. Turn left and walk along the railway line until you see the next clue.
5. Turn right. Go to the nearest crossroads and turn right. The treasure is under the second tree on the right.
6. Go straight on over the bridge to the crossroads.
7. Walk back and read the last clue again.
8. Go into the nearest field. The next clue is under the first tree on the right.

9. This clue says the same as number 13.
10. Walk along the river bank to the next bridge.
11. Get on the next train; get off at the other station.
12. There's a train coming. Turn to your left and get off the railway line.
13. Go under the bridge. The next clue is just on the other side.
14. Turn left and go to the second tree on the right.
15. Go straight out of the field and take the shortest way to the river by road. The next clue is at the crossroads.
16. You're lost.

## 2 Describe the route you took to the treasure.

*I went straight over the bridge to the crossroads; then I turned left and went to the second tree on the right; ...........*

## 3 Look at the summary on page 153 with your teacher.

# Knowing about the future

## A This is going to be my room

**1** What are your plans for this evening? Are you going to do any of these things?

| | |
|---|---|
| write letters | see a film |
| play cards | see friends |
| watch TV | wash your hair |
| listen to music | study |

**Examples:**

*'I'm going to write letters.'*
*'I'm not going to watch TV.'*

**2** This is going to be your house. It isn't finished yet. Look at the plan and decide what the various rooms are going to be and how you are going to furnish them. Include some or all of the following: kitchen, bathroom(s), toilet(s), bedrooms, living room, dining room, study, playroom, and any other rooms that you want. If you haven't got enough rooms, put on another floor.

When you have finished, work with another student and tell him/her what the rooms are going to be. Example:

*'This is going to be the kitchen.'*

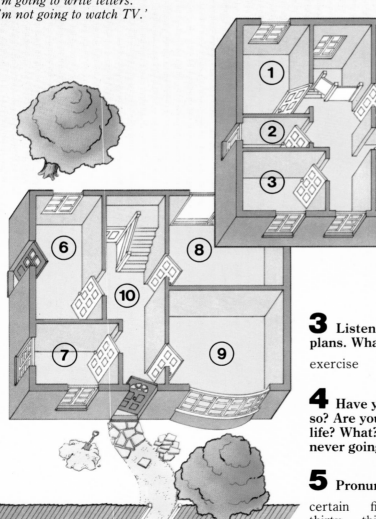

**3** Listen to some people talking about their plans. What do you think these words mean?

exercise   kid   shout   couple   less

**4** Have you got any plans for the next year or so? Are you going to make any changes in your life? What? Think of something that you are never going to do again in your life.

**5** Pronunciation. Say these words.

| | | | | | |
|---|---|---|---|---|---|
| certain | first | bird | dirty | stir | third |
| thirty | thirsty | shirt | turn | hurt | Thursday |
| work | word | world | worst | | |
| learn | heard | early | year | | |

102

# B  It's going to rain

**1** Look at the pictures. What is going to happen? (If you don't know the words, use your dictionary or ask your teacher.)

**2** Read the advertisement. Then make up advertisements yourselves (working in groups) to get people to join your holiday trip.

HOLIDAY IN SCOTLAND
We are organizing a holiday walking tour in the North of Scotland.
We are going to cover 150 miles of mountainous country in ten days.
It's going to be hard work.
It's going to be tough.
You're going to be wet, cold and tired a lot of the time.
But it's going to be fun!
If you are young and fit, and if you like beautiful places – why not join us? Cost £38 inclusive.
For more details, write Box 1346, *Edinburgh Times*.

We are organizing a trip to
...................................... .
We are going to ............
...................................... .
It's going to be ............
...................................... .
It's going to be ............
...................................... .
And/But it's going to be ..
...................................... .
If you are ...................
...................................... ,
...................................... , and
...................................... ,
why not join us?
Cost: £ ............ inclusive.

**3** Mime a person who is going to do something. The other students will try to say what you are going to do.

> You're going to swim.

# C Why? To...

**1** You go to a university to study.
Why do you go to these places?

**2** Can you make five more sentences like these?

*'People don't go to Nigeria to ski.'*
*'People don't go to Iceland to drink wine.'*

**3** Why are you learning English?

**4** Mr Andrews is an English tourist who is travelling to Eastern Europe tomorrow. Just now he's having breakfast at home. After breakfast, he's going out to do a lot of things. (For example, he's going to Harrods to buy a suitcase.) Look at the pictures, and then write a paragraph to say where he's going and why. Connect your sentences with *First of all, then, and then, after that, next, tomorrow.*

Where?      Why?

# D   To and -ing

## INFINITIVE WITHOUT *TO* (**Examples:** go, speak)

### Used after 'auxiliary verbs':

| | |
|---|---|
| can | *I can speak German.* |
| could | *Could you speak more slowly?* |
| will | *It will rain tomorrow.* |
| should | *You should be at home.* |
| do | *Does he smoke?* |
| | *Don't stop.* |
| let's | *Let's have a drink.* |

## INFINITIVE WITH *TO* (**Examples:** to go, to speak)

### Used in many kinds of sentence. After:

| | |
|---|---|
| something | *Would you like something to eat?* |
| nothing | *There's nothing to do.* |
| anything | *Have you got anything to drink?* |
| I'm sorry | *I'm sorry to trouble you.* |

### Also used after many verbs:

| | |
|---|---|
| would like | *Would you like to dance?* |
| would love | *I'd love to speak German.* |
| hope | *I hope to see you soon.* |
| want | *I don't want to go home.* |
| have | *You have to change at the next station.* |

### And used to say why we do things:

*'Why did you come here?' 'To see you.'*

## *-ING* FORM (**Examples:** going, speaking)

### Used in many kinds of sentence. After some verbs:

| | |
|---|---|
| like | *I like speaking French.* |
| love | *I love going to the theatre.* |
| hate | *I hate waiting for people.* |

### And after all prepositions:

| | |
|---|---|
| after | *After seeing the doctor I felt better.* |
| before | *Before going to bed I usually read the paper.* |
| for | *Thank you for inviting me.* |
| at | *She's good at swimming.* |
| without | *Can you get there without changing?* |

### And in the Present Progressive tense:

*'What are you doing?' 'I'm writing letters.'*

**1** Put in the infinitive with or without *to*.

1. Can you ............? (swim)
2. Have you got anything ............? (read)
3. Could I ............ to Lucy? (speak)
4. I don't ............. (understand)
5. I'd like ............ you again. (see)
6. I hope ............ to America in May. (go)
7. It takes a long time ............ English. (learn)
8. Let's ............. (dance)
9. Why don't we ............ a drink? (have)

**2** Put in the infinitive or the *-ing* form.

1. Would you like ............? (dance)
2. Do you like ............? (dance)
3. Can you ............ chess? (play)
4. Thank you for ............ me. (help)
5. I'm very bad at ............. (ski)
6. You can't live without ............. (eat)
7. How do you ............ 'please'? (pronounce)
8. Could you ............ me the time? (tell)
9. I love ............. (cook)
10. My husband can't ............. (cook)

**3** Listen to the song. When the recording stops, say what is coming next.

**4** Look at the summary on page 154 with your teacher.

# Feelings

## A I feel ill

1. I've got a cold.

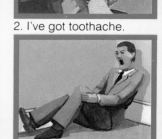

2. I've got toothache.

3. I've got a temperature.

4. I've got flu.

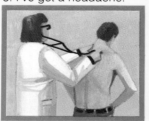

5. I've got a headache.

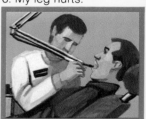

6. My leg hurts.

a. Why don't you go home and lie down?

b. Why don't you take an aspirin?

c. Why don't you see the doctor?

d. Why don't you see the dentist?

**1** Match the letters and the numbers. You can use a dictionary.

**2** Ask and answer.

*'How do you feel?'*
*'I'm very hungry, and my arm hurts a bit.'*

**3** Listen to the dialogue. Then change some of the words and practise it with a partner. Your teacher will help you.

WOMAN: Good morning, Mr Culham. How are you?
MAN:　I feel ill.
WOMAN: I *am* sorry. What's the matter?
MAN:　My eyes hurt, and I've got a bad headache.
WOMAN: Well, why don't you take an aspirin?
MAN:　That's a good idea.

**4** At the doctor's. Write the other half of this dialogue. Work in groups if you can. Your teacher will help you.

DOCTOR: Good morning. What's the problem?
YOU:　Well, ................................... .
DOCTOR: I see. Does it / Do they hurt very badly?
YOU:　................................... .
DOCTOR: How long have you had this?
YOU:　................................... .
DOCTOR: Yes, right. I'd like to examine you, then. Mmm... Mmm...
YOU:　...................................?
DOCTOR: No, it doesn't look too bad. Here's a prescription for some medicine. Phone me if you're not better by the day after tomorrow.
YOU:　................................... .
DOCTOR: Goodbye.
YOU:　................................... .

**5** Ask your teacher how to say three other words you can use at the doctor's.

# B It frightens me

**1** Choose one of the pictures above. Ask other students: *'How do you feel about this picture?'*
Examples of answers:

*'It frightens me.'*   *'It depresses me.'*   *'It makes me angry.'*   *'I think it's lovely.'*   *'I think it's interesting.'*   *'I think it's disgusting.'*   *'I don't like it much.'*

**2** Think of four other things and write about your feelings towards them. You can use words from Exercise 1 or from the box. Examples:

*Unemployment worries me.*
*I think cigarettes are disgusting.*

| worries | happy | funny | wonderful |
| bores | unhappy | pretty | beautiful |
| | | stupid | exciting |
| | | nice | |

**3** Survey. Ask other students about one of the things you wrote about. Report the results to the class.

**4** Put a word or words in each blank. Then listen and practise.

TOM: ..........., Jill. How ...........?
JILL: ........... depressed.
TOM: I ............ What's the matter?
JILL: ........... boyfriend isn't here. ...........
America.
TOM: Oh dear! Well, ........... you ........... to
........... dinner with us tonight?
JILL: That's ........... nice of you, Tom. ...........,
I ............
TOM: See you ........... seven o'clock, then. ...........
JILL: ............

**5** Work with a partner. Make and practise a new conversation using words from the lesson.

# C Do you like your boss?

WE ASKED THREE PEOPLE:

Celia

I really like my boss. She's a lovely person, very easy to work for, very fair. She always asks what I think before she changes anything. If there's a problem, we solve it together. She never gets angry. I trust her, and she trusts me. It's a pleasure to work for her.

George

I get on all right with my ............ He ............ worry about ............ details of ............ work; he's ............ fair, and ............ gives me a lot ............ freedom. ............ like that. It ............ me a bit angry when he ............ me more work ............ I can ............ . I don't ............ he understands that parts ............ my job ............ very difficult. But on the whole, I don't ............ we ............ on too badly.

Lesley

I .............................. job, .............................. can't stand
.............................. difficult
..............................;
.............................. talk
.............................. really listen. And he's not
.............................. : *he* can make mistakes, and that's all right; but
.............................. , he .............................. angry. It
when .............................. *me* angry when he changes his mind about
really .............................. again and again. I can't leave
.............................. right now, .............................. really fed up.

**1** Read Celia's text; put one word in each blank in George's text; put one or more words in each blank in Lesley's text. You can use a dictionary.

**2** Think of one person you know (boss/ sister/uncle etc.). Write four sentences about how you get on with that person. Try to use words from the texts.

**3** Work in groups. Each person reads the sentences from Exercise 2 and the others ask questions. Some words you can use in your questions:

| easy/difficult to talk to | angry | problems |
| trust | freedom | listen | mistakes |

**4** Copy this list. Then listen, and mark off each expression when you hear it.

in a pub     he's smashing     sense of humour
easy to get on with     very fair     when I first came
everything that I needed to know
wasn't unfair     I made mistakes     very good to me

**How does the person feel about her boss – more like Celia, more like George or more like Lesley?**

# D Love at first sight

**1** Which people do you think go with text 1? Which people do you think go with text 2? Write a text for the third couple.

A    B    C

D    E    F

1. We've been married for 15 years. We met on holiday in the mountains, and it was love at first sight. We've had a few problems over the years, but we're still happy to be together. We do nearly everything together.

2. We both had terrible first marriages. It made us appreciate each other much more. We've been together for four years now. We don't spend all our time together, but we're happy to share a lot of things.

**2** How does -e change the pronunciation?

| WITHOUT -e: fat  cat  am  plan  hat | NOW PRONOUNCE: man same take that |
| WITH -e:  gate  late  name  plane  hate | make bad lemonade bale safe tap tape |
| WITHOUT -e: sit  in  begin  if  swim | NOW PRONOUNCE: fit inside still mile hid |
| WITH -e:  invite  fine  wine  wife  time | ride tide like pipe strip |
| WITHOUT -e. stop  top  not  hot  clock | NOW PRONOUNCE: job stone rose God |
| WITH -e:  hope  home  note  nose  smoke | joke dome bone on spot coke |
| WITHOUT -e: bus  run  pub  sun  just | NOW PRONOUNCE: much fuse cube cub |
| WITH -e:  excuse  June  tube  rude  use | fuss tune gun fun duke luck |
| EXCEPTIONS:   some   come   one   have   give   live   love | |

**3** Look at the summary on page 155 with your teacher.

# Movement and action

## A How to get from A to B

**1** Travelling. You can often say the same thing in two different ways. Try to complete the table.

| | |
|---|---|
| ride | = go on horseback |
| ............ | = go on foot |
| drive | = go ............ |
| fly | = ............ |
| cycle | = ............ |

**Other expressions:**

hitchhike    go by boat    go by bus
go by train    go by motorbike

**2** A man makes a journey across Britain. He uses several different forms of transport. Listen, and say how he is travelling.

**3** This is the story of the man's journey. Fill in the missing words.

| | | | | | |
|---|---|---|---|---|---|
| boat | broke down | drove | fast | flew |
| hitchhiking | motorbike | one day | packed |
| rode | so | so | so | train | walked |
| when | who | worse | | | |

Paul Lewis lives in the south of England; he has a brother John, ............ lives on Barra, a small island near the west coast of Scotland. ............ a friend of John's telephoned to say John was very ill, and he wanted Paul with him. Paul ............ as ............ as he could, caught the next ............ to Heathrow Airport, and ............ to Glasgow. There he hired a car and ............ off to catch the ............ for Barra. Unfortunately the car ............ three miles from the ferry. Paul tried ............, but he couldn't get a lift, ............ he ............ to the ferry. ............ he landed on Barra the island's one taxi was not there, ............ he borrowed a horse and ............ to John's house. John was much ............, ............ Paul took his brother's ............ and went to call the doctor.

**4** Talk about a journey that you have made. **Example:** *'When I was 16 I cycled from Munich to Cologne.'*

# B Like lightning

**1** Match the words and the pictures.

| a cheetah     a glacier |
| lightning     a racehorse |
| a racing pigeon     a rhinoceros |
| a salmon     a sprinter |
| a wasp     a snail |

**2** Lightning is the fastest of the things in the pictures. Which do you think is the next fastest? Which do you think is the slowest? Put them in order of speed.

**3** Match the nouns and verbs, and guess the speeds. Example:

*Lightning travels at 140,000 kilometres a second.*

> A cheetah     A glacier
> Lightning     A racehorse
> A rhinoceros
> A racing pigeon
> A salmon     A sprinter
> A wasp     A snail

> flies    gallops    runs
> moves    crawls
> swims    travels

> at

> 50 metres per hour.     176kph.
> 36kph.     19kph.     56kph.
> 3mm per hour.     100kph.
> 36kph.     68kph.     140,000kps.

**4** How fast do you think you walk, run, cycle, drive, read, breathe,...?

**5** Listening for information. Copy the table. Listen to today's results from the Fantasian National Games, and note the times and speeds.

| EVENT | TIME | SPEED |
|---|---|---|
| Men's 100m | | |
| Women's marathon | | |
| Women's 100m swimming (freestyle) | | |
| Downhill Alpine skiing | | |

**6** Listening to fast speech. What is the second word in each sentence? (Contractions like *what's* count as two words.)

## C If you press button A,...

**1** *Get* has several different meanings. Put these sentences in groups, according to the meaning of *get*.

What time do you usually get up?
It's getting late.
My English is getting better.
Where can I get some cigarettes?
John got into his car and drove away.

It takes me an hour to get to work.
I get a letter from my mother every week.
The housing problem is getting worse.
If you go to the shops, can you get me some bread, please?
You've got beautiful eyes.

**2** How does the machine work?

If you — press push pull turn — button lever handle — A B D F C E — you get — a cup of coffee. a packet of cigarettes. a flower. music. a surprise. an electric shock.

**3** Where did you get...? Ask and answer.
Examples:

*'Where did you get your shoes?' 'In Tokyo.'*
*'Where did you get your dictionary?' 'At the University Bookshop.'*
*'Where did you get that watch?' 'From my father.'*

**4** Put in *on, off, into, out of, up.*

1. What time did you get ............ this morning?
2. She got ............ her car and drove away.
3. I got ............ my car and walked up to the front door.
4. 'Why are you late?' 'I got ............ the wrong bus.'
5. We have to get ............ at the next stop.

**5** Put in suitable adjectives.

1. If you don't eat, you get ............ .
2. If you eat too much, you get ............ .
3. If you don't drink, you get ............ .
4. If you drink too much alcohol, you get ............
5. If you run a long way, you get ............ .
6. If you go out in the rain without an umbrella, you get ............ .
7. If you go out in the snow without a coat, you get ............ .
8. In the evening, when the sun goes down, it gets ............ .
9. We are all getting ............ .

# D Please speak more slowly

**1** How are the people speaking? Listen to the recording, and choose one adverb for each sentence.

| | |
|---|---|
| coldly | kindly |
| sleepily | angrily |
| happily | |

**2** Now listen to the next five sentences, and find more adverbs to say how the people are speaking.

**3** Now practise speaking in all ten ways. Then work with a partner and make up a short conversation. Speak coldly, or angrily, or fast, . . . ; the other students must say how you are speaking.

**4** Choose a verb and an adverb, and demonstrate or mime the action (for example: *walk happily; drink slowly*). The other students must say what you are doing, and how you are doing it.

> write    eat    drink    walk
> sing    speak    run    drive
> fly    sleep    cook    dance
> swim    smoke    type    wash
> play (the guitar/piano/etc.)

> fast    slowly    loudly    quietly
> happily    unhappily    angrily
> sleepily    coldly    kindly
> shyly    noisily    badly

> You're walking happily.

**5** Adjective or adverb?

1. I'm very ........... with you. (angry/angrily)
2. She spoke to me ............. (angry/angrily)
3. I don't think your mother drives very ............. (good/well)
4. You've got a ........... face. (nice/nicely)
5. I play the guitar very ............. (bad/badly)
6. It's ........... cold. (terrible/terribly)
7. Your father's got a very ........... voice. (loud/loudly)
8. Why are you looking at me ...........? (cold/coldly)
9. You speak very ........... English. (good/well)
10. You speak English very ............. (good/well)

**6** Put the adverb in the right place.

1. He read the letter without speaking. (slowly)

   *He read the letter slowly without speaking.*

2. She speaks French. (badly)
3. I like dancing. (very much)
4. Please write your name. (clearly)
5. You should eat your food. (slowly)
6. She read his letter. (carefully)
7. I said 'Hello' and walked away. (coldly)

**7** Spelling. Look carefully at these adverbs.

| | | | |
|---|---|---|---|
| badly | quietly | nicely | completely |
| angrily | happily | carefully | comfortably |

**Now make adverbs from these adjectives.**

| | | | |
|---|---|---|---|
| warm | great | extreme | sincere |
| hungry | lazy | real | terrible |

**8** Look at the summary on page 155 with your teacher.

# Parts

## A Education

**GCE:** General Certificate of Education.
There are two parts:
**O Level** (Ordinary Level), taken at age 16.
**A Level** (Advanced Level), taken at age 18.

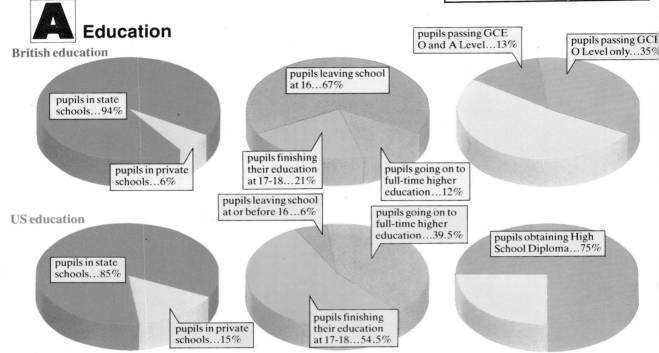

British education

- pupils in state schools...94%
- pupils in private schools...6%
- pupils leaving school at 16...67%
- pupils finishing their education at 17-18...21%
- pupils leaving school at or before 16...6%
- pupils passing GCE O and A Level...13%
- pupils passing GCE O Level only...35%
- pupils going on to full-time higher education...12%

US education

- pupils in state schools...85%
- pupils in private schools...15%
- pupils finishing their education at 17-18...54.5%
- pupils going on to full-time higher education...39.5%
- pupils obtaining High School Diploma...75%

**1** Look at the statistics. Then complete the following sentences with some of these words and expressions.

| very few | not many | some | two thirds |
|---|---|---|---|
| three quarters | nearly all | more | |
| far more | nearly | less than | |

1. ............ British pupils go to private schools.
2. ............ British pupils go to state schools.
3. ............ American than British pupils go to private schools.
4. About ............ of British pupils leave school at 16.
5. ............ American pupils leave school at 16.
6. ............ 40% of American pupils go on to full-time higher education.
7. ............ 15% of British pupils go on to full-time higher education.
8. ............ of American pupils obtain the High School Diploma.
9. ............ British pupils pass GCE A Level.
10. ............ American than British pupils go on to full-time higher education.

**2** Listen to the six recorded sentences and say whether they are true or false.

**3** Say something about the educational system in your country. Is it different from the British and American systems?

**4** Now listen to some sentences about you and the other students.
If you think they are true, write 'true'; if not, write 'false'.
If you are not sure, write 'probably' or 'probably not'.
If you have no idea, write 'don't know'.
Examples:

1. 'You all speak some English.' *True*
2. 'Most of you smoke.' *False*
3. 'Nearly all of you are over 18.' *Don't know*

**5** Ask questions to find out the truth about the statements in Exercise 4.
Tell the other students what you have found out, or make a statistical diagram and show it to the other students.

# B | At the top on the left

## 1 What can you see in the pictures? Write sentences.

Picture 1 is
Picture 2 is
Picture 3 is
Picture 4 is
Picture 5 is
Picture 6 is

the top of ............
the side of ............
the front of ............
the back of ............
the bottom of ............
the corner of ............

## 2 Use *at the top/bottom/front/back/side(s)* in your answers to these questions.

1. Where is 6 on a clock face? Where is 12?
2. Where are the doors of a car? Of a house?
3. Where is north on a map? Where is south?
4. Where is the engine of a train?
5. Where does a bus driver sit?
6. Where is the garage of a house, usually?
7. Where are your ears?
8. Where is the index in a book?
9. Where are the stars on an American flag?

## 3 Read the description of the first picture; complete the description of the second picture; and write the third description yourself.

There's a big circle. Inside the circle at the top there's a small triangle. On the right at the side there are two small circles. On the left at the side there's a dot, and there's another dot at the bottom. In the middle there's a small square.

There's a big ............
............ the triangle at the
............ there's a ............
............ On the ............ at the
............ there are three
............; ............ the
............ ............ the ............
there are four ............ Outside
the triangle on the ............
............ ............ ............
circle, and there's a small
............ near the bottom
left-hand ............ .

## 4 Listen to the recording and draw the picture.

## 5 Draw a picture. Describe it to another student and see if he/she can draw it.

# C The beginning of the end

## 1 At the beginning; in the middle; at the end.

A is at the beginning of the alphabet; M is in the middle of the
  alphabet; W is near the end of the alphabet. Where is C?
  Where is K? Where is Z?
Where is Unit 1 in this course? Unit 16? Unit 27? Unit 32?
When is June? June 15th? Three a.m.? Three p.m.? Monday?
When do people usually have soup?
When do you buy a train ticket?
When do you clap in a theatre?
When do the lights go out in a cinema?
When is a person's funeral?

## 2 Listen to the sounds and answer the questions.

1. When was the music loud? When was it quiet? When did somebody say 'Hello'?
2. Describe what you heard.
3. When did the telephone ring? When did somebody say 'Hello'? What else did you hear? When?
4. When did you hear the baby? When did somebody say 'Hello'? When did somebody say 'Goodbye'?
5. When did you hear the wind? the motorbike? the water? the door? What did you hear in the middle?
   Did the train come before or after the clock?
6. Describe what you heard. About how long did it last?

## 3 Pronunciation. How many words? Listen to each sentence, and write the number of words you hear.

## 4 Where does the stress come in these words? Where does the sound /ə/ come?

machine    about    usually
mother    photograph    alphabet
pronunciation    China    Japan
remember    cinema    America

---

'In the beginning was the Word.'    The Bible

'In my beginning is my end.'    T.S. Eliot

'This is the beginning of the end.'    Talleyrand, 1812

'This is not the end. It is not even the
beginning of the end. But it is, perhaps,
the end of the beginning.'    Churchill, 1942

'Where shall I begin, please,
Your Majesty?' he asked.
'Begin at the beginning,' the
King said, gravely, 'and go on
till you come to the end.
Then stop.'    Carroll, *Alice in Wonderland*

'I like a film to have a
beginning, a middle
and an end, but not
necessarily in that order.'

Jean-Luc Godard

# D What happened next?

**1** Here is a story called *The Medical Book.*
Put the pictures in the right order.
Which picture comes first?
Which one is next?
Which one comes after that? ...
Which one is last?

A

B

C

D

E

F

G

H

I

**2** Read the text, and put in the following words and expressions.

| next | first | after that | then | finally |
|------|-------|------------|------|---------|

GETTING UP

............ I get out of bed, go to the toilet, and wash and shave. ............ I get dressed and brush my hair. ............ I go downstairs and pick up the post and the newspaper. ............ I have a long slow breakfast while I read my letters and the paper. ............ I brush my teeth, put on my coat and leave for work.

**3** Watch the actions, and then write down what happened. Try to use some of these words and expressions.

| first | then | next | after that | finally |
|-------|------|------|------------|---------|

**4** Put the parts of the story in order.

1. 'Didn't I tell you
2. 'Take it to the zoo,'
3. said the man,
4. a man was walking in the park
5. 'I did,'
6. He still had the penguin.
7. 'and he liked it very much.'
8. answered the policeman.
9. and asked what to do.
10. he asked.
11. 'Now I'm taking him to the cinema.'
12. the policeman saw the man again.
13. when he met a penguin.
14. Next day
15. to take that penguin to the zoo?'
16. So he took it to a policeman
17. One day

**5** Look at the summary on page 156 with your teacher.

117

# Predictions

## A Are you sure you'll be all right?

### 1 Study and practise the dialogue.

A: I'm going to hitchhike round the world.
B: Oh, that's very dangerous.
A: No, it isn't. I'll be all right.
B: Where will you sleep?
A: Oh, I don't know. In youth hostels. Cheap hotels.
B: You'll get lost.
A: No, I won't.
B: You won't get lifts.
A: Yes, I will.
B: What will you do for money?
A: I'll take money with me.
B: You haven't got enough.
A: I'll find jobs.
B: Well, ... are you sure you'll be all right?
A: Of course I'll be all right.

### 2 Complete these dialogues.

A: I'm ............ be a racing driver.
B: Oh, that's ............. .
A: No, it ............. .
B: You'll crash. ............ get killed.
A: No, ............. .
B: You ............ find a job.
A: Yes, ............ . I'm a good driver.
B: Are you sure ............? 
A: Of course ............. .
———◇———
A: ............ a doctor.
B: ............ have to study for seven years.
A: Yes, I know. I don't mind.
B: ............ finish.
A: Yes, I ............. .
B: ............ have a really hard life.
A: Yes, but it' ............ interesting.
B: ............ have to work very long hours.
A: I know. But I' ............ enjoy it.
B: OK. If that's what you want.
A: It is.

### 3 Write and pronounce the contractions.

I will *I'll*
you will
he will
she will
it will
we will
they will
I will not *I won't*
you will not
it will not

### 4 Work with another student. Make up a short conversation beginning:

A: 'I'm going to get married.'
or A: 'I'm going to work in a circus.'
or A: 'I'm going to be a teacher.'
or A: 'I'm going to ski down Everest.'
or A: 'I'm going to be a pilot.'

### 5 Listen. Which sentence do you hear?

1. I stop work at six.
   I'll stop work at six.
2. You know the answer.
   You'll know the answer.
3. I have coffee for breakfast.
   I'll have coffee for breakfast.
4. You have to change at Coventry.
   You'll have to change at Coventry.
5. I drive carefully.
   I'll drive carefully.
6. I know you like my brother.
   I know you'll like my brother.

### 6 Where will you be this time tomorrow? What will you be doing? Example:

*'I'll be at home. I'll be watching TV.*

# B What will happen next?

**1** Find out what these words mean. Ask your teacher or use a dictionary.

| | | |
|---|---|---|
| dead | prison | revolution |
| employer | royal | |
| procession | Duke | palace |
| mistress | famous | |
| successful | heart | |
| refuse(*verb*) | cousin | |

**2** Read the 'opera synopsis'. Then close your book and see how much you can remember.

**3** You are at a performance of the opera *Death in Paris*. It is the interval between the second and third acts. What do you think will happen in the third act?

**4** Listening. Listen to the recording. When each sentence stops, say what you think the next word will be. Example:

1. 'What's the time?' 'Three...'
*'I think the next word will be 'o'clock'.'*

# DEATH IN PARIS

### An Opera in Three Acts
### by
### Zoltan Grmljavina

### SYNOPSIS

## ACT ONE

Anna, a beautiful 18-year-old girl, works in a shop in the old town of Goroda, in Central Moldenia. Her parents are dead; her lover, Boris, is in prison for revolutionary activities; her employer is very unkind to her. She dreams of a happier life. One day a royal procession passes in the street. The Grand Duke sees Anna and falls in love with her. He sends for her; when she goes to the palace he tells her that she must become his mistress. If not, Boris will die. Anna agrees. Boris is released from prison; in a letter Anna tells him that she can never see him again. Boris leaves Moldenia.

## ACT TWO

Three years have passed. Anna and the Duke are in Paris. The Duke is dying – he has only six months to live – but the doctors have not told him. Only Anna knows the truth. One day, Anna is walking in the Tuileries when a man stops her. It is Boris. He tells her that he is now a famous artist, rich and successful. He is married to a Frenchwoman, Yvette; but in his heart he still loves Anna. 'Come away with me', he says. Anna refuses, and Boris says that he will do something terrible. At this moment, Yvette joins them. Boris tells Yvette that Anna is his cousin from Moldenia, but Yvette does not believe him.

## ACT THREE

Anna and

# C What do the stars say?

**AQUARIUS** (Jan 21–Feb 18) An old friend will come back into your life, bringing new problems. Don't make any quick decisions.

**PISCES** (Feb 19–Mar 20) In three days you will receive an exciting offer. But your family will make difficulties.

**ARIES** (Mar 21–Apr 20) Money will come to you at the end of the week. Be careful – it could go away again very fast!

**TAURUS** (Apr 21–May 21) You will have trouble with a child. Try to be patient. You will have a small accident on Sunday – nothing serious.

**GEMINI** (May 22–June 21) This will be a good time for love, but there will be a serious misunderstanding with somebody close to you. Try to tell the truth.

**CANCER** (June 22–July 22) You will meet somebody who could change your life. Don't be too cautious – the opportunity won't come again.

**LEO** (July 23–Aug 23) Something very strange will happen next Thursday. Try to laugh about it.

**VIRGO** (Aug 24–Sept 23) This will be a terrible week. The weekend will be the worst time. Stay in bed on Sunday. Don't open the door. Don't answer the phone.

**LIBRA** (Sept 24–Oct 23) There will be bad news the day after tomorrow; but the bad news will turn to good.

**SCORPIO** (Oct 24–Nov 22) You will make an unexpected journey, and you will find something very good at the end of it.

**SAGITTARIUS** (Nov 23–Dec 21) You will have trouble with a person who loves you; and you will have help from a person who doesn't.

**CAPRICORN** (Dec 22–Jan 20) A letter will bring a very great surprise, and some unhappiness, but a good friend will make things better.

**1** Read your horoscope with a dictionary. Memorize it – and see if it comes true.

**2** Work with some more people who have the same sign as you, if possible.
Write a new horoscope for your sign, and for another one.

**3** Make some predictions about football matches. Examples:

*'Arsenal will beat Liverpool 3 – 1 next Saturday.'*

Or make predictions about some other sport. Or about the 'top twenty' records. Example:

*'"Baby come here" will be number one.'*
*'"Get out of my heart" will go up three places.'*

Remember your predictions and see if they come true.

**4** How old will you be in the year 2000? What do you think you will be like? What about other people in the class? Write a few sentences about the future of yourself and some of the other students.

# D A matter of life and death

**1** You are at the North Pole. Your tractor and radio transmitter have broken down and you cannot repair them. You have to walk 100 miles (160 km) to the nearest camp. You have enough warm clothing and boots; you also have the following things on the tractor, but you can't carry them all. What will you take? Choose carefully – it's a matter of life and death.

matches (20g)
saucepan (500g)
large water bottle (empty 300g, full 2.5kg)
tent (4kg)
tin-opener (80g)
first aid kit (500g)
backpack (1.5kg)
sunglasses (40g)
gas cartridges (300g each)

ten blankets (1.5kg each)
gas cooker (1.2kg)
toothbrush (10g)
20m of rope (3kg)
compass (50g)
small radio receiver (1.2kg)
rifle and ammunition (6.9kg)
30kg of tinned food
ten signal flares (1.5kg)

**2** Look at the summary on page 157 with your teacher.

# Useful; useless

## A All you need is love

## 1 Who needs what? Make some sentences.

| People | Men |
| Women | Babies |
| Fish | Cars |
| Animals | Gardens |

need
don't need

people. men.
women. babies. fish.
bicycles. cars. milk.
love. freedom. water.
petrol. oil. sleep.
politicians. books.
clothes.

## 2 What do people need in life? Make a list of ten things. You can use your dictionary. What do *you* need now?

## 3 How important are these things to you? Very important? Quite important? Not very important?
Which is the most important? Which is the least important? List them in order of importance, and compare lists with three other students.

| a car | children | TV | interesting work |
| money | love | freedom | nice clothes |
| music | friends | books | time to be alone |

## 4 We asked some people to name two things each that were very important to them. Which ten different things do you think they named?

| family | home | life | freedom | car |
| friends | friendship | music | happiness |
| money | rugby boots | work | health |

Now listen, and see if you were right. Try to note how many times each thing is named as important.

## 5 Listen to the short extracts from songs, and try to write the words.

"*He's got toothache, a sprained ankle, a bad back, gout, influenza, a broken arm and an ulcer and he's just hoping someone will ring him up and ask him how he is.*"

KenPyne

122

# B  Is it useful?

**1** Work in pairs. Which of these subjects are necessary for a good education? Which are useful? Which are useless? Make three lists to read to the class.

| | | | |
|---|---|---|---|
| reading | spelling | mathematics | history |
| geography | sports | physical sciences | |
| literature | biology | religious education | |
| English | typing | cookery | |

**2** Work in groups. Choose four jobs and decide which school subjects are
✓✓ necessary   ✓ useful   ✗ useless
for each one.

| | Architect | Banker | Doctor | Engineer | Farmer | Journalist | Photographer | Secretary | Businessman or Businesswoman |
|---|---|---|---|---|---|---|---|---|---|
| Mathematics | | | | | | | | | |
| English | | | | | | | | | |
| Geography | | | | | | | | | |
| Latin | | | | | | | | | |
| History | | | | | | | | | |
| Typing | | | | | | | | | |
| Biology | | | | | | | | | |
| Art | | | | | | | | | |
| Physics | | | | | | | | | |
| Chemistry | | | | | | | | | |

**3** These people are beginning their last two years of school. They can each take five of the subjects from Exercise 2. Which five subjects should each one take? Why?

1. Pat wants to be a doctor. She enjoys languages.
2. John would like to be an architect. He does well in sciences, but they are not his favourite subjects.
3. Judy will own and manage the family farm when she is older. She likes to travel.
4. Tom plans to be a journalist. He would like to write about international politics.

**4** Complete the sentences.

1. A photographer uses a camera to take pictures with.
2. A journalist uses a tape recorder to record interviews with.
3. ..............................................................................
4. An architect ............ drafting table ............ draw plans on.
5. ........................................................ in.
6. ............ tractors ............ plough fields ............ .
7. ..............................................................................
8. ............ a barn ............ keep cows ............ .

1. A photographer takes pictures with a camera.
2. ..............................................................................
3. Farmers milk cows with milking machines.
4. ..............................................................................
5. ............ secretary takes notes in shorthand.
6. ..............................................................................
7. Nurses take temperatures ............ thermometers.
8. ..............................................................................

tractor   barn   field

shorthand   thermometer   tape recorder

# C It's useless (part one)

ASSISTANT: Good afternoon, madam. Can I help you?
CUSTOMER: Yes, I'd like to see the manager, please.
ASSISTANT: Furniture, madam? Second floor.
CUSTOMER: No, the *manager. Ma-na-ger.*
ASSISTANT: Oh, I *am* sorry. I thought you said furniture.
CUSTOMER: That's all right. But can I see the manager, please?
ASSISTANT: Well, I'm afraid he's *very* busy just now. Have you an appointment?
CUSTOMER: No, I haven't. I want to make a complaint.
ASSISTANT: A complaint. Oh, I see. Well, I'll just see if he's free.

**1** Listen to the conversation. Then decide whether these sentences are true or false.

1. The conversation happens in the afternoon.
2. The customer wants to buy furniture.
3. She is on the second floor.
4. The assistant doesn't understand what she wants.
5. The woman hasn't got an appointment.
6. The manager is not free.
7. The woman wants to complain about something.

**2** Study the conversation, and practise it in pairs.

**3** Work with a partner, and make up a short conversation which includes a misunderstanding and an apology. You can use one of these sentences if you like.

I thought you said Thursday.
I thought you said goodbye.
I thought you said five pence.
I thought you said five o'clock.
I thought you said steak.
I thought you were talking to me.

**4** Stress. List each of these words under one of the stress patterns. Then pronounce them.

happiness      furniture      animal
bicycle        afternoon      literature
mathematics    appointment

| ■ □ □ | □ □ ■ | □ ■ □ |
|---|---|---|
| *manager* | *engineer* | *already* |

124

# D It's useless (part two)

MANAGER: Good afternoon, madam. I understand you have a complaint.
CUSTOMER: Yes, I've got a problem with this hair-drier.
MANAGER: I'm sorry to hear that. What's the trouble?
CUSTOMER: Well, first of all, I ordered it two months ago and it only arrived yesterday.
MANAGER: Oh dear. That's very strange.
CUSTOMER: Well, it's probably because you addressed it to Mr Paul Jones at 29 Cannon Street.
I'm *Mrs Paula* Jones, and my address is *39* Cannon Street.
MANAGER: Well, I'm really sorry about that, madam. We do…
CUSTOMER: And secondly, I'm afraid it's useless. It doesn't work.
MANAGER: Doesn't work?
CUSTOMER: No. It doesn't work. It doesn't dry my hair. When I switch it on, it just goes 'bzzzzz', but it doesn't get hot at all.
MANAGER: Well, I really am very sorry about this, madam. I do apologize. We'll be happy to replace the drier for you. Or we'll give you a refund instead, if you prefer.
CUSTOMER: And thirdly,…

**1** Listen to the conversation. Find out what the new words and expressions mean.

**2** Practise the conversation with a partner.

**3** Stress. Listen carefully to these questions, and then write answers to them (beginning *No, ·····*). When you have done that, practise saying the questions and answers.

1. You've got *two* sisters, haven't you?
   *No, just one*

2. You've got two *sisters*, haven't you?
   *No, two brothers*

3. You work in London, don't you?
4. Is that Mary's father?
5. Did you say you had a new red Lancia?
6. Do you need English for your work?

**Now listen to this question. You will hear it three times, with three different stresses. Can you write suitable answers (a different answer each time)?**

7. Would you like me to telephone Peter and Anne?

**4** Many words in English can be used in different ways. For example, *rain* can be used as a noun (*Look at the rain!*), or as a verb (*It will rain tomorrow*); and *open* can be used as a verb (*Is it OK if I open the window?*) or an adjective (*the open door*). Can you find any words in the conversation that can be used in different ways like this? Can you think of any other words?

**5** Which of these words can be used in more than one way?

| arrive | answer | orange | music | phone |
|---|---|---|---|---|
| cold | pub | hear | clean | bath | change | warm |

**6** A *shop* that sells *shoes* is a *shoe shop* (not a ~~*shoes shop*~~). How can you say:

a *lamp* in the *street*       a *shop* that sells *books*
the *door* of a *garage*      a *window* in a *kitchen*
a *wheel* of a *bicycle*      a *horse* that runs in *races*
a *bottle* for *beer*            a *boy* who brings *newspapers*
a *race* for *horses*          a *finger* you put a *ring* on

**7** Prepare and practise a sketch about a complaint.

**8** Look at the summary on page 158 with your teacher.

# Self and others

## A Do it yourself

falling in love
with each other
× ×

a woman looking at herself in a mirror

a man looking at himself in a mirror

**1** Work with two other people. Tell them to do things, like this:

> Look at   Sing to
> Touch    Talk about
> Talk to
> Shake hands with

> yourselves.
>
> each other.

**2** You can look at yourself, or you can look at somebody else.
You can talk to yourself or to somebody else.
Can you do all these things to somebody else *and* to yourself?

hurt     visit     fall in love with     photograph
marry     employ     teach     wash
think about     telephone

**3** Draw small pictures for these situations.

He's looking at her.
She's looking at herself.
They're looking at each other.
He's not looking at her, he's looking at somebody else.

**4** Alan bought six things yesterday – three for himself and three for somebody else. Which were which, do you think?

a bunch of roses          a bottle of perfume
a train ticket            a stamp
a cigar                   a birthday card

**5** Do you do these things yourself, or does somebody else do them for you? Examples:

*1. 'I do the ironing myself.'*
*2. 'Somebody else does the decorating.'*

1. ironing   2.decorating  3. cooking   4. washing

5. cleaning      6. washing-up      7. shopping

**Now listen to an English person answering the same questions.**

**6** Do you prefer to do these things by yourself or with somebody else?

listen to music          go to the cinema
go shopping              go on holiday
have lunch               go for a walk

# B  Shall I open it for you?

**1** Put the sentences in the right pictures.

| | |
|---|---|
| Shall I open it for you? | Shall I get it for you? |
| Shall I carry something for you? | I'll go, shall I? |
| Shall I have a look? | I'll answer it, shall I? |

**2** What do you think the answers will be?
Can you complete the sentences?

1. 'Can I take your coat?'
   'Oh, thank you. Here ............ .............'
   'No, thanks. I'll keep ............ on. I'm .............'

2. 'Shall I make you a cup of tea?'
   'Thank you very much. I'd love .............'
   'Not just now, thanks. I'm not .............'
   'I'd prefer coffee, if you've ............ .............'

3. 'Would you like some toast?'
   'No, nothing ............ ............, thanks.'
   'Yes, ............ love ............. Thank you.'
   'No, I've just ............ ............, thanks.'

4. 'Would you like to go and see a film this evening?'
   'That would be very .............'
   'I'd love ............. ............ time?'
   'Not this evening, ............ Perhaps ............ time?'

5. 'Would you like to dance?'
   'Thanks. ............ love .............'
   'Not ............ now, thanks. I'm a bit .............'

6. 'Shall I help you to carry that?'
   'That's ............ kind of you. Thank you.'
   'No, thanks. I can do it .............'

**3** Prepare your answers to the following questions.
Then close your book, listen to the recording and answer.

Can I take your coat?
Shall I make you a cup of tea?
Would you like some toast?
Would you like to go and see a
  film this evening?
Shall I put the TV on?
Would you like a drink?

Would you like to have a rest?
Would you like to see my family
  photos?
Shall I telephone the station for
  you?
Would you like to wash your
  hands?

**4** Prepare a conversation with another student (an offer
and an answer). Act the conversation *without speaking*.
The other students will try to decide what the words are.

**5** Listen to the sentences. How many words do you hear?
Write the first three words in each sentence. (Contractions
like *that's* or *I'd* count as two words.)

127

# C Whose is that?

## 1 Match the pictures and the sentences.

Mine, mine, all mine!    Is this yours?    It's his.
Our baby's prettier than theirs.    Whose is that?
My feet are smaller than hers.    At last! It's ours!

## 2 *His, hers* or *not sure*?

## 3 Exchange possessions with other students.
Then ask '*Whose is this?*'
See if everybody can remember.

## 4 Put in *my, mine, your, yours, his, her, hers, our, ours, their* or *theirs*.

1. 'Excuse me, that's ............ coat.'
2. 'Oh, is it? I'm sorry – I thought it was ............'
3. We've got the same kind of house as Mr and Mrs Martin, but ............ is a bit bigger than ours.
4. Could we have ............ bill, please?
5. 'Is that Jane's cat?' 'No, this one's white. ............ is black.'
6. 'Have you seen ............ new motorbike?' 'Oh, it isn't ............. He's just borrowed it.'
7. 'When's ............ birthday?' 'December 15th.' 'Really? Mine's the day before ............'
8. Mary and ............ boyfriend are taking ............ holiday in June – the same time as we're taking ............. Why don't we all go together?

## 5 Listen to the conversations and fill in the table.

| | George | Keith | Pat | Edna | Jane |
|---|---|---|---|---|---|
| The car belongs to | | | | | |
| The new trousers belong to | | | | | |
| The glasses belong to | | | | | |
| The dictionary belongs to | | | | | |
| The plate belongs to | | | | | |
| The history book belongs to | | | | | |

128

# D Do you ever talk to yourself?

**1** Survey of people's personal habits.
a. Make sure you know how to answer all the following questions in English.
b. Choose one of the questions (a different one from the other students), and go round the class asking the others your question.
c. Work out a statistic. Examples:

*'Seventy-five per cent of the students in this class eat between meals.'*
*'Three students out of eight talk to themselves.'*

1. Do you lie in bed after waking up?
2. Do you like people to talk to you before breakfast?
3. What do you have for breakfast?
4. Do you get dressed before or after breakfast?
5. What do you wear in bed?
6. Do you eat between meals?
7. Do you ever shut yourself in the bathroom to get away from people?
8. Do you ever talk to yourself?
9. Do you daydream at work?
10. Do you have arguments with other people in your head?
11. Are you more awake in the morning or the evening?
12. Do you sing in the bath?
13. Do you wash your clothes yourself, or does somebody else wash them for you?
14. Do you often cook for yourself?
15. Do you like shopping?
16. Do you do your ironing yourself, or does somebody else do it for you?
17. Do you eat in bed?
18. Do you like looking in a mirror?

**2** Put in one of these words.

| somebody | anybody | everybody | nobody |
|----------|---------|-----------|--------|
| something | anything | everything | nothing |
| somewhere | anywhere | everywhere | nowhere |

1. ........... can speak all the languages in the world.
2. I think there's ........... at the door.
3. 'Where are my keys?' 'I've seen them ..........., but I can't remember where.'
4. Have you got ........... to eat?
5. Does ........... know where I put my glasses?
6. You can find Coca Cola ............
7. I need ........... to read – have you got a paper?
8. I'm bored – there's ........... to do.
9. ........... needs love.
10. My wife and I always tell each other ............
11. 'Come and see a film with us.' 'I don't want to go ...........'
12. 'Where can I find a good job with plenty of money and no work?' '...........'

**3** Vocabulary revision. Which word is different?
Can you find a word that names all the others?
Example:

sofa    chair    table    wall    bed
*'Wall is different. The others are all furniture.'*

1. tea    coffee    bread    milk
2. cooking    cleaning    ironing    dancing
3. green    big    blue    red
4. fair    blond    red    green    grey    dark
5. water    meat    bread    fish
6. car    sheep    train    bicycle
7. Aries    Taurus    Mars    Gemini
8. July    Christmas    March    January
9. book    letter    TV    newspaper
10. uncle    friend    sister    mother

**4** Now listen to a little boy doing the same kind of exercise. Which word does he choose each time, and what is his reason?

1. horse    dog    book    cat
2. fish    lamb    beef    pork
3. apple    orange    pear    banana
4. knife    fork    cup    spoon
5. run    walk    chair    jump
6. TV    grass    flower    tree
7. shout    cry    laugh    sing
8. Mummy    Daddy    Mark    Granny
9. watch    calculator    shirt    camera

**5** Look at the summary on page 159 with your teacher.

129

# Revision and fluency practice

## A You have to throw a six

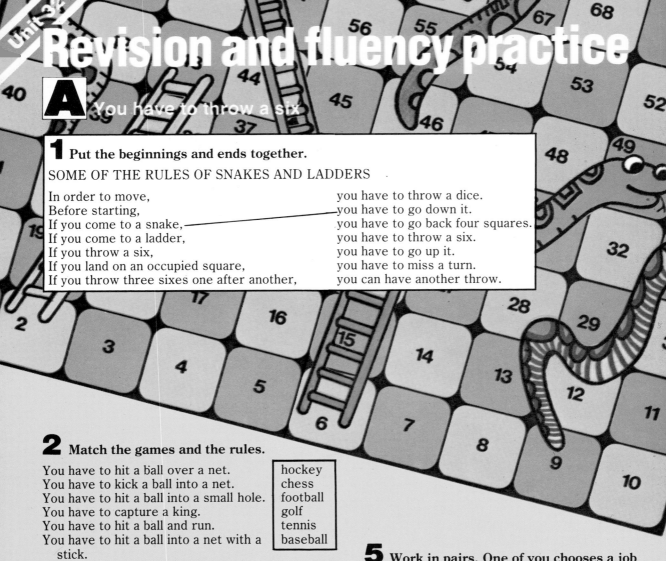

**1** Put the beginnings and ends together.

SOME OF THE RULES OF SNAKES AND LADDERS

| | |
|---|---|
| In order to move, | you have to throw a dice. |
| Before starting, | you have to go down it. |
| If you come to a snake, | you have to go back four squares. |
| If you come to a ladder, | you have to throw a six. |
| If you throw a six, | you have to go up it. |
| If you land on an occupied square, | you have to miss a turn. |
| If you throw three sixes one after another, | you can have another throw. |

**2** Match the games and the rules.

You have to hit a ball over a net.
You have to kick a ball into a net.
You have to hit a ball into a small hole.
You have to capture a king.
You have to hit a ball and run.
You have to hit a ball into a net with a
    stick.

hockey
chess
football
golf
tennis
baseball

**3**

In Britain: nobody has to do military service;
you don't have to carry an identity card; you have
to drive on the left; you don't have to pay to go into
a museum; you have to be over 18 to drink alcohol
in a pub or bar; you have to pay for your drink
before you drink it.
**What is the situation in your country?**

**4** What do these people have to do?

A person who wants to travel by air.
A secretary.
Somebody who wants to cook a steak.
A person who wants to get into a university in your
    country.
A person who wants a driving licence.

**5** Work in pairs. One of you chooses a job
from this list (without telling his/her partner).

| | | | |
|---|---|---|---|
| architect | lorry driver | coal miner | doctor |
| electrician | photographer | businessman | |
| secretary | pilot | teacher | shop assistant |

**The other asks the following questions, and
then tries to guess his/her partner's job.**

Do you have to get up early?
Do you have to get your hands dirty?
Do you have to travel?
Do you have to think a lot?
Do you have to study for a long time to learn the job?
Do you have to work long hours?
Do you have to handle money?
Do you have to work with people a lot?
Do you have to write letters?
Do you have to use machines?

# B Get it right

## 1 What's wrong with the pictures? Examples:

*'The elephant's ears should be bigger.'*
*'The elephant's ears are too small.'*

## 2 Put the parts of the story in the right order. Three of the parts don't belong in the story.

1. 'Excuse me,
2. and ordered a whisky.
3. and then he thought
4. so he stood up
5. The gorilla gave him the money
6. but he gave him the whisky,
7. A gorilla went into a pub,
8. There was silence for a few minutes,
9. 'Is it raining?'
10. so he asked him for £5.
11. but you don't often see a gorilla in a pub.'
12. and then the barman said
13. 'with whisky at £5 a glass.'
14. and started drinking.
15. 'It's not surprising,' said the gorilla
16. The barman was rather surprised,
17. on the other side of the room
18. 'Gorillas probably don't understand much about money,'
19. walked up to the bar,

## 3 In these sentences, some of the words are wrong. Listen to the recording and correct them.

1. 'Hello, Mary, I'm home,' said John, speaking rather fast.
2. 'John!' she said happily. 'Listen – a wonderful thing has happened.'
3. 'How's the car running?' 'Very well.'
4. 'Is your bath OK?' 'Just fine.'
5. 'Peter – how are you?' she said coldly.
6. Sally knocked at the door. 'Come in!' said a friendly voice.
7. It's a fine day. The sun's shining.
8. Little birds are singing.
9. Robert walked quietly up the stairs.

## 4 Put the correct verb form into the sentences.

1. I ............ 800km yesterday. (drive)
2. We ............ our cousins from Scotland last weekend. (see)
3. 'How was the party?' 'Very nice. George ............ too much.' (drink)
4. That child ............ too much TV. (watch)
5. I don't like ............ (shop)
6. 'Would you like a cigarette?' 'No, thanks. ............'
   (I don't smoke / I'm not smoking)
7. What ............ tomorrow? (do you do / are you doing)
8. 'Shall we go out?' 'No, ............' (it rains / it's raining)
9. I ............ Mary for about six years. (know)
10. ............ you ever ............ Japanese food? (have, eat)

## 5 Make questions.

1. where | your wife | work?
2. your children | live | with you?
3. you ever | been | to Africa?
4. Mary and Peter | going to | get married?
5. What | your father | do | when he stops work next year?
6. why | you | come home so late last night?

# C Listening and cartoons

**1** Listen to the song, and try to write down the words.

**2** Listen to the story, and imagine or mime the actions.

**3** Say what you think of the cartoons. Examples:

*'I think number one's funny. I don't like number two.'*
*'I don't understand number three. I like number four best.'*

"Bills, bills, bills..."
**1**

**2**

MY SON IS INNOCENT
**3**

ACKEN.
"I'M SURE YOU AND MOTHER WILL LIKE EACH OTHER."
**4**

'Well, If I Called the Wrong Number, Why Did You Answer the Phone?'
**5**

# D A visitor

Prepare and practise a sketch with two or three other students. In your sketch, you must have:

**A VISITOR**

This can be a person, an animal, a thing… You decide.

**A PROBLEM**

**For example:**

Somebody is feeling ill.
There isn't enough money.
Somebody or something is lost.
Somebody can't understand.
Somebody is unhappy.
Something is broken.
Something doesn't work.

**ROLES**

**Decide who you are.**

What are your names?
What are your jobs?
What kind of personalities do you have?

**'LANGUAGE FUNCTIONS'**

**Use English to do some of these things:**

buy
sell
ask for information
explain
complain
invite
greet
suggest
order
offer
describe
compliment
compare
give instructions
express feelings
predict
borrow
lend
get to know somebody
give opinions
thank
apologize

**A PLACE**

**Where are you? Perhaps:**

at an airport
on a plane
on a ship
on a train
in a hotel
in a restaurant
in a shop
at a station
in a park
in the street
at home
in a pub
at the doctor's
at the North Pole
in the Sahara Desert
on the moon

# Unit 1

## Grammar and structures

### *Be*: singular

| | | |
|---|---|---|
| I am /aɪ æm/<br>you are /ju: ɑ:(r)/<br>he is /hi: ɪz/<br>she is /ʃi: ɪz/<br>it is /ɪt ɪz/<br>my name is /maɪ neɪm ɪz/ | I'm /aɪm/<br>you're /jɔ:(r)/<br>he's /hi:z/<br>she's /ʃi:z/<br>it's /ɪts/<br>my name's /maɪ neɪmz/ | am I...? /æm aɪ/<br>are you...? /ɑ: ju:/<br>is he...? /ɪz hi:/<br>is she...? /ɪz ʃi:/<br>is it...? /ɪz ɪt/<br>is your name...? /ɪz jɔ: neɪm/ |

| | | |
|---|---|---|
| I am not /aɪ æm nɒt/<br>you are not /ju: ɑ: nɒt/<br>he is not /hi: ɪz nɒt/<br>she is not /ʃi: ɪz nɒt/<br>it is not /ɪt ɪz nɒt/<br>my name is not /maɪ neɪm ɪz nɒt/ | I'm not /aɪm nɒt/<br>you aren't /ju: ɑ:nt/<br>he isn't /hi: ɪznt/<br>she isn't /ʃi: ɪznt/<br>it isn't /ɪt ɪznt/<br>my name isn't /maɪ neɪm ɪznt/ | 'Is your/his/her name Mark Perkins?'<br>'Yes, it is.' (Yes, it's.) 'No, it isn't.'<br><br>'Are you Fred Andrews?'<br>'Yes, I am.' (Yes, I'm) |

### Possessives

| What is<br>What's | your<br>his<br>her | name? |
|---|---|---|

| My<br>Your<br>His<br>Her | name is<br>name's | John.<br>Catherine.<br>Mary Lake.<br>Harry Brown. |
|---|---|---|

### *From*

'Where are you from?' 'I'm from Canada.'

| Where is<br>Where's | he<br>she | from? |
|---|---|---|

| He<br>She | 's<br>is | from Scotland. |
|---|---|---|

I speak a little English.

Here's my bus.

## Words and expressions to learn

### Nouns

name /neɪm/
first name /'fɜ:st neɪm/
surname /'sɜ:neɪm/
Britain /'brɪtn/
England /'ɪŋglənd/
Scotland /'skɒtlənd/
the United States /ðə ju:'naɪtɪd 'steɪts/

### Pronouns

my /maɪ/
your /jɔ:(r)/
his /hɪz/
her /hə(r), hɜ:(r)/
I /aɪ/
you /jʊ, ju:/
he /hi, hi:/
she /ʃi, ʃi:/
it /ɪt/

### Verbs

am /əm, æm/
are /ə(r), ɑ:(r)/
is /ɪz/
speak /spi:k/

### Adjectives

British /'brɪtɪʃ/
English /'ɪŋglɪʃ/
Scottish /'skɒtɪʃ/
American /ə'merɪkən/

### Question-words

what /wɒt/
where /weə(r)/
how /haʊ/

### Numbers

1 one /wʌn/
2 two /tu:/
3 three /θri:/
4 four /fɔ:(r)/
5 five /faɪv/
6 six /sɪks/
7 seven /'sevən/
8 eight /eɪt/
9 nine /naɪn/
10 ten /ten/
11 eleven /ɪ'levən/
12 twelve /twelv/
13 thirteen /θɜ:'ti:n/
14 fourteen /fɔ:'ti:n/
15 fifteen /fɪf'ti:n/
16 sixteen /sɪks'ti:n/
17 seventeen /sevən'ti:n/
18 eighteen /eɪ'ti:n/
19 nineteen /naɪn'ti:n/
20 twenty /'twenti/

## Other words and expressions

and /ənd, ænd/
from /frəm, frɒm/
not /nɒt/
here /hɪə(r)/
a little /ə ˈlɪtl/
Hello. /həˈləʊ/
Hi. /haɪ/

How are you? /haʊ ˈɑ: jʊ/
Fine, thanks. /ˈfaɪn ˈθæŋks/
How do you do? /ˈhaʊ djə ˈdu:/
Goodbye. /gʊdˈbaɪ/
Bye. /baɪ/
See you. /ˈsi: jʊ/
Thank you. /ˈθæŋkjʊ/

Yes. /jes/
No. /nəʊ/
I don't know. /aɪ dəʊnt ˈnəʊ/
Excuse me. /ɪksˈkju:z mi /
(I'm) sorry. /(aɪm) ˈsɒri/
That's right. /ˈðæts ˈraɪt/
Oh. /əʊ/

# Unit 2

## Grammar and structures

### Asking and answering

What do you do?

| I'm a | doctor. |
|---|---|
| | dentist. |
| | teacher. |
| | student. |
| | housewife. |

| I'm an | artist. |
|---|---|
| | engineer. |
| | electrician. |

(I'm doctor.)

'How old are you?' 'I'm thirty-six.'

## Words and expressions to learn

### Nouns

> **Learn three or more of these:**
> teacher /ˈti:tʃə(r)/
> artist /ˈɑ:tɪst/
> shop assistant /ˈʃɒp əˈsɪstənt/
> secretary /ˈsekrətri/
> doctor /ˈdɒktə(r)/
> dentist /ˈdentɪst/
> student /ˈstju:dnt/
> engineer /endʒəˈnɪə(r)/
> electrician /ɪlekˈtrɪʃən/
> housewife /ˈhaʊswaɪf/

morning /ˈmɔ:nɪŋ/
afternoon /ɑ:ftəˈnu:n/
evening /ˈi:vnɪŋ/
night /naɪt/
nationality /næʃəˈnæləti/

### Adjectives

married /ˈmærɪd/
single /ˈsɪŋgl/
divorced /dɪˈvɔ:st/
different /ˈdɪfrənt/
good /gʊd/
old /əʊld/

### Numbers

30 thirty /ˈθɜ:ti/
31 thirty-one /θɜ:tiˈwʌn/
40 forty /ˈfɔ:ti/
50 fifty /ˈfɪfti/
60 sixty /ˈsɪksti/
70 seventy /ˈsevənti/
80 eighty /ˈeɪti/
90 ninety /ˈnaɪnti/
100 a hundred /ə ˈhʌndrəd/

### Other words and expressions

or /ɔ:(r)/
well /wel/
Good morning (afternoon etc.).
I'm very well, thank you.
not bad /nɒt ˈbæd/
How old are you? /haʊ ˈəʊld a: jʊ/
How do you spell ...?
    /ˈhaʊ djʊ ˈspel/
write /raɪt/
a, an /ə, ən/
do /də, du:/
Mr /ˈmɪstə(r)/
Mrs /ˈmɪsɪz/
Ms /mɪz or /məz/
Miss /mɪs/

# Unit 3

## Grammar and structures

### Be: plural

| | | |
|---|---|---|
| we are /wi: ə(r), wi: ɑ:(r)/ | | we're /wɪə(r)/ |
| you are /ju: ə(r), ju: ɑ:(r)/ | | you're /jɔ:(r)/ |
| they are /ðeɪ ə(r), ðeɪ ɑ:(r)/ | | they're /ðeə(r)/ |

| |
|---|
| are we...? /ɑ: wi:/ |
| are you...? /ɑ: ju:/ |
| are they...? /ɑ: ðeɪ/ |

| | | |
|---|---|---|
| we are not /wi: ə nɒt/ | | we aren't /wi: ɑ:nt/ |
| you are not /ju: ə nɒt/ | | you aren't /ju: ɑ:nt/ |
| they are not /ðeɪ ə nɒt/ | | they aren't /ðeɪ ɑ:nt/ |

### Have got

I have got (I've got) two brothers.
Bruce and Sally have got one daughter. They've got one daughter.
'Have you got any children?' 'Yes, I have.' (Yes, I've.)
'No, I haven't.'

### Noun plurals

| Singular | Plural |
|---|---|
| parent | parents |
| boy | boys |
| family | families |
| boss | bosses |
| wife | wives |
| child | children |

### Possessive: 's

John's father. (father's John   the John's father)
Joyce's (/'dʒɔɪsɪz/) mother.

### Personal pronouns and possessives

| Singular | Plural | |
|---|---|---|
| I | we | |
| you | you | |
| he | | personal pronouns |
| she | they | |
| it | | |
| my | our | |
| your | your | |
| his | | possessives |
| her | their | |
| its | | |

### Time

What time is it?   It's ten past seven.
It's a quarter past seven.
It's half past seven.
It's ten to eight.
It's eight o'clock.

'Who is John's wife?' 'Mary is.' (Mary's.)

John is tall. John and Mary are tall. (talls)

## Words and expressions to learn

### Nouns

child /tʃaɪld/
  (plural children /'tʃɪldrən/)
boy /bɔɪ/
girl /gɜ:l/
family /'fæməli/
  (plural families /'fæməlɪz/)
friend /frend/
boyfriend /'bɔɪfrend/
girlfriend /'gɜ:lfrend/
boss /bɒs/ (plural bosses /'bɒsɪz/)
question /'kwestʃən/
age /eɪdʒ/
time /taɪm/

| Learn seven or more of these: | |
|---|---|
| wife /waɪf/ (plural wives /waɪvz/) | nephew /'nevju:/ |
| husband /'hʌzbənd/ | niece /ni:s/ |
| brother /'brʌðə(r)/ | aunt /ɑ:nt/ |
| sister /'sɪstə(r)/ | uncle /'ʌŋkl/ |
| son /sʌn/ | cousin /'kʌzən/ |
| daughter /'dɔ:tə(r)/ | parent /'peərənt/ |
| mother /'mʌðə(r)/ | |
| father /'fɑ:ðə(r)/ | |
| grandmother /'grændmʌðə(r)/ | |
| grandfather /'grændfɑ:ðə(r)/ | |
| grandson /'grændsʌn/ | |
| granddaughter /'grænddɔ:tə(r)/ | |

## Pronouns

we /wi:/
they /ðeɪ/

## Possessives

our /aʊə(r)/
their /ðeə(r)/

## Adjectives

> **Learn five or more of these:**
> tall /tɔ:l/
> fair /feə(r)/
> dark /dɑ:k/
> pretty /'prɪti/
> short /ʃɔ:t/
> good-looking /gʊd'lʊkɪŋ/
> strong /strɒŋ/
> young /jʌŋ/
> intelligent /ɪn'telɪdʒənt/
> fat /fæt/
> slim /slɪm/

## Other words and expressions

have (got) /həv, hæv (gɒt)/
who /hu:/
very /'veri/
fairly /'feəli/
not very /'nɒt veri/
sit down /sɪt 'daʊn/
please /pli:z/
of course /əv 'kɔ:s/
aren't you? /'ɑ:nt jʊ/
Pardon? /'pɑ:dn/
too /tu:/
but /bət, bʌt/
a moment /ə 'məʊmənt/
half /hɑ:f/
a quarter /ə 'kwɔ:tə(r)/
past /pɑ:st/
to /tu:/
o'clock /ə'klɒk/
What time is it? /wɒt 'taɪm ɪz ɪt/
What does ... mean? /'wɒt dəz ... 'mi:n/

# Unit 4

## Grammar and structures

Newcastle is **a** large town in **the** north of England.

a small town (a town small)

**on** the beach **in** Paris **at** the Kremlin

That's in Brazil, **isn't it**?

## Words and expressions to learn

### Nouns

the north /ðə 'nɔ:θ/
the south /ðə 'saʊθ/
the east /ði 'i:st/
the west /ðə 'west/
the north-east
the north-west
town /taʊn/
village /'vɪlɪdʒ/
city /'sɪti/ (*plural* cities /'sɪtɪz/)
coast /kəʊst/
capital /'kæpɪtl/
tourist /'tʊərɪst/
centre /'sentə(r)/
mountain /'maʊntɪn/
beach /bi:tʃ/
population /pɒpjʊ'leɪʃn/
place /pleɪs/

### Adjectives

large /lɑ:dʒ/
small /smɔ:l/
industrial /ɪn'dʌstrɪəl/
nice /naɪs/
exciting /ɪk'saɪtɪŋ/
noisy /'nɔɪzi/
quiet /'kwaɪət/

### Prepositions

in /ɪn/
on /ɒn/
at /ət, æt/
near /nɪə(r)/
of /əv, ɒv/

### Numbers

101 a hundred and one
132 a hundred and thirty-two
300 three hundred (three hundreds)
1,000 a thousand /'θaʊznd/
1,400 one thousand four hundred
1,000,000 a million /'mɪljən/

### Other words and expressions

the /ðə, ði/
about /ə'baʊt/
that /ðæt/
I think /aɪ 'θɪŋk/
Where in ...? /'weər ɪn/

# Unit 5

## Grammar and structures

### *There is* / *There are*

There is a big kitchen in the flat.
 (/ðərɪzə.../)
There's a small bathroom.
 (/ðəzə.../)
There are two bedrooms.
 (/ðərə.../)
Is there a...? (/'ɪz ðərə.../)
Are there...? (/'ɑ: ðə.../)
There is not... (/ðərɪznɒt/)
There isn't... (/ðər'ɪznt/)
There are not... (/ðərənɒt/)
There aren't... (/ðər'ɑ:nt/)
Yes, there is. (Yes, there's.)
 No, there isn't.
Yes, there are. No, there aren't.

### Simple Present tense

| | |
|---|---|
| I live | I work |
| you live | you work |
| he/she live**s** | he/she work**s** |
| we live | we work |
| you live | you work |
| they live | they work |

### Prepositions of place

**in** Birmingham **in** Queen Street
 **in** a flat
**at** 17 Queen Street, Birmingham
**on** the fourth floor

### Telephones

Can I take a message?
Could I speak to Sally?
'Who's that?' 'This is John.'
Could you tell Mary that Bill called?

### Noun plurals

| | Singular | Plural |
|---|---|---|
| *Regular:* | flat | flats |
| | room | rooms |
| | family | families |
| | address | addresses |
| *Irregular:* | man | men |
| | woman | women |
| | child | children |
| | person | people |
| | wife | wives |

## Words and expressions to learn

### Nouns

house /haʊs/
 (*plural* houses /'haʊzɪz/)
room /ru:m/
flat /flæt/
floor /flɔ:(r)/
ground floor /graʊnd flɔ:(r)/
first floor /fɜ:st flɔ:(r)/
street /stri:t/
road /rəʊd/
address /ə'dres/
telephone /'telɪfəʊn/
phone /fəʊn/
number /'nʌmbə(r)/
(tele)phone number
food /fu:d/
man /mæn/ (*plural* men /men/)
woman /'wʊmən/
 (*plural* women /'wɪmɪn/)
person /'pɜ:sən/
 (*plural* people /'pi:pl/)

| Learn four or more of these: |
|---|
| bedroom /'bedru:m/ |
| kitchen /'kɪtʃɪn/ |
| bathroom /'bɑ:θru:m/ |
| toilet /'tɔɪlɪt/ |
| living room /'lɪvɪŋ ru:m/ |
| window /'wɪndəʊ/ |
| door /dɔ:(r)/ |
| stairs /steəz/ |
| wall /wɔ:l/ |
| garage /'gærɑ:ʒ/ |

| Learn four or more of these: |
|---|
| furniture /'fɜ:nɪtʃə(r)/ |
| chair /tʃeə(r)/ |
| bed /bed/ |
| cooker /'kʊkə(r)/ |
| sofa /'səʊfə/ |
| fridge /frɪdʒ/ |
| armchair /'ɑ:mtʃeə(r)/ |
| television /telɪ'vɪʒn/ |
| TV /ti:'vi:/ |
| cupboard /'kʌbəd/ |
| bath /bɑ:θ/ |
| wardrobe /'wɔ:drəʊb/ |
| table /'teɪbl/ |

### Verbs

live /lɪv/
work /wɜ:k/
can /kən, kæn/
could /kʊd/

### Adjectives

big /bɪg/
clean /kli:n/
next /nekst/

### Numbers

1st first /fɜ:st/
2nd second /'sekənd/
3rd third /θɜ:d/
4th fourth /fɔ:θ/
5th fifth /fɪfθ/
6th sixth /sɪksθ/
7th seventh /'sevənθ/
8th eighth /eɪtθ/
9th ninth /naɪnθ/

### Other words and expressions

this /ðɪs/
well /wel/
Love /lʌv/
speaking /'spi:kɪŋ/
wrong number /rɒŋ 'nʌmbə(r)/
one moment /wʌn 'məʊmənt/
Can I take a message?
 /'kæn aɪ 'teɪk ə 'mesɪdʒ/
You're welcome. /jɔ: 'welkəm/
double /'dʌbl/

# Unit 6

## Grammar and structures

### Simple Present tense

| | | |
|---|---|---|
| I start<br>you start<br>he/she/it starts<br>we start<br>they start | do I start?<br>do you start?<br>does he/she/it start?<br>do we start?<br>do they start? | I do not (don't) start<br>you do not (don't) start<br>he/she/it does not (doesn't) start<br>we do not (don't) start<br>they do not (don't) start |

*Spelling:* he starts   he stops   he works   he likes   he loves
          he finishes   he watches   he goes   he does   he studies
*Pronunciation:* -(e)s = /z/: loves   goes   sells   repairs
           -(e)s = /s/: works   gets   likes
           -es = /ɪz/: finishes   watches
           do /duː, də/   does /dʌz, dəz/   don't /dəʊnt/   doesn't /'dʌznt/
'He works on Saturdays.' 'Does he work on Saturdays?' (Do he works? Does he works?)
'Yes, he does.' 'No, he doesn't.'
'Do you work on Saturdays?' (Work you?) 'Yes, I do. I work on Saturday mornings.'

'Do you like dogs?' (Do you like the dogs?) 'Yes, I do.' (Yes, I like.) 'No, I don't.'
Everybody likes children. (Everybody like . . .) Nobody likes Harry. (Nobody like . . .)

---

## Likes and dislikes

I like my work. I like it. I like skiing (dancing, watching football). I like it.

I like dogs. I like them.

George likes Mary, but Mary doesn't like him.

'Do you like Ann?' 'Yes, I like her very much.'

I like skiing very much. (I like very much skiing.) I quite like tennis. I neither like nor dislike football. I don't like rugby very much at all. Do you? I like skiing best.

---

## Have

I have breakfast at eight o'clock.

| | |
|---|---|
| I have<br>you have<br>he/she has | we have<br>you have<br>they have |

## Adding *-ing*

cook – cooking   watch – watching
work – working   read – reading

dance – dancing (danceing)
write – writing (writeing)

shop – shopping (shoping)
travel – travelling (traveling)

---

'**How** do you get to work?' '**By** car/train/bus/bicycle.' '**On** foot.'
'(At) **what time** do you get up?' '**At** six o'clock.'

---

# Words and expressions to learn

### The days of the week

Monday /'mʌndi/
Tuesday /'tjuːzdi/
Wednesday /'wenzdi/
Thursday /'θɜːzdi/
Friday /'fraɪdi/
Saturday /'sætədi/
Sunday /'sʌndi/

## Nouns

**Learn six or more of these:**
breakfast /'brekfəst/
lunch /lʌntʃ/
supper /'sʌpə(r)/
book /bʊk/
tea /ti:/
coffee /'kɒfi/
shop /ʃɒp/
music /'mju:zɪk/
maths /mæθs/
dog /dɒg/
whisky /'wɪski/
letter /'letə(r)/
the sea /ðə 'si:/
cat /kæt/
clothes /kləʊðz/
job /dʒɒb/
work /wɜ:k/
tennis /'tenɪs/
newspaper
  /'nju:speɪpə(r)/
language /'læŋgwɪdʒ/
beer /bɪə(r)/
wine /waɪn/
garage /'gærɑ:ʒ/

## Verbs

**Learn fifteen or more of these:**
like /laɪk/
dislike /dɪs'laɪk/
love /lʌv/
hate /heɪt/
watch /wɒtʃ/
cook /kʊk/
dance /dɑ:ns/
go /gəʊ/
start /stɑ:t/
open /'əʊpn/
have (lunch etc.) /hæv/
  (he/she has /hæz/)
stop /stɒp/
drink /drɪŋk/
play /pleɪ/
get up /get 'ʌp/
read /ri:d/
do /du:/
shop /ʃɒp/
travel /'trævl/
sell /sel/

## Other words and expressions

**Learn nine or more of these:**
only /'əʊnli/
not much /nɒt 'mʌtʃ/
not . . . at all /nɒt . . . ə'tɔ:l/
him /hɪm/
her /hə(r), hɜ:(r)/
it /ɪt/
them /ðəm, ðem/
after /ɑ:ftə(r)/
(At) what time . . . ?
  /(ət) wɒt 'taɪm/
What sort of . . . ? /wɒt 'sɔ:t əv/
from . . . until /frəm . . . ən'tɪl/
nobody /'nəʊbədi/
everybody /'evribɒdi/
quite /kwaɪt/
neither . . . nor
  /'naɪðə(r) . . . nɔ:(r)/
it depends /ɪt dɪ'pendz/
by bus /baɪ 'bʌs/
by car /baɪ 'kɑ:(r)/
at the weekend /ət ðə wi:'kend/
interested in /'ɪntrəstɪd ɪn/
on holiday /ɒn 'hɒlədi/
watch TV /wɒtʃ ti:'vi:/
both /bəʊθ/

# Unit 7

## Grammar and structures

### Uncountable and countable nouns

| U | C |
|---|---|
| water | a car |
| (a water) | two cars |
| (two waters) | (a cars) |
| | |
| bread | a litre |
| (a bread) | two litres |
| (two breads) | (a litres) |

Your hair is too long. (Your hairs are . . . )

### Quantifiers

| U | C (plural) |
|---|---|
| how much water? | how many cars? |
| too much water | too many cars |
| not much water | not many cars |
| some water | some cars |
| any water | any cars |
| a lot of water | a lot of cars |
| enough water | enough cars |
| | |
| a litre **of** water | a kilo **of** bananas |
| half a litre | half a kilo |

### *Some* and *any*

| YES | ? | NO |
|---|---|---|
| There is some water. | Is there any water? | There isn't any water. |
| There are some cows. | Are there any cows? | There aren't any cows. |

## Articles

Food costs a lot of money. (The food . . .)
Oranges are £1.40 a kilo. (The oranges . . .)

Furniture is expensive. (The furniture . . . Furniture are . . .)

## Was and were

| I was | we were |
| you were | you were |
| he/she/it was | they were |

I was in Patterson's yesterday.
Bananas were £2.25 a kilo.

# Words and expressions to learn

## Nouns

gram /græm/
kilo(gram) /'ki:ləʊ/
litre /'li:tə(r)/
money /'mʌni/
price /praɪs/
pound /paʊnd/
penny /'peni/ (plural pence)
memory /'meməri/
tree /tri:/
grass /grɑ:s/
toothpaste /'tu:θpeɪst/
shaving cream /'ʃeɪvɪŋkri:m/
perfume /'pɜ:fju:m/
light /laɪt/
hair /heə(r)/ (hairs)

**Learn three or more of these:**

tomato /tə'mɑ:təʊ/ (plural tomatoes)
egg /eg/
water /'wɔ:tə(r)/
steak /steɪk/
potato /pə'teɪtəʊ/ (plural potatoes)
cheese /tʃi:z/
bread /bred/
orange /'ɒrɪndʒ/
milk /mɪlk/
banana /bə'nɑ:nə/

**Learn two or more of these:**

cow /kaʊ/
pig /pɪg/
chicken /'tʃɪkɪn/
sheep /ʃi:p/ (plural sheep)
horse /hɔ:s/
duck /dʌk/

## Other words and expressions

terrible /'terəbl/
yesterday /'jestədi/
I know /aɪ 'nəʊ/
Do you know? /dʒʊ 'nəʊ/
I don't remember.
    /aɪ dəʊnt rɪ'membə(r)/
I don't understand.
    /aɪ dəʊnt ʌndə'stænd/
much /mʌtʃ/
many /'meni/
how much /'haʊ 'mʌtʃ/
how many /'haʊ 'meni/
too much /'tu: 'mʌtʃ/
too many /'tu: 'meni/
a lot of /ə 'lɒt əv/
enough /ɪ'nʌf/
some /səm, sʌm/
any /eni/
listen (to) /lɪsn (tə, tu:)/
try /traɪ/

# Unit 8

# Grammar and structures

## Prepositions

**at** a restaurant    **at** the cinema
**at** the swimming pool    **at** the disco
**at** school (at the school)    **at** home (at the home)

**by** the stairs          **on** the right    **on** the left

**near** the police station    **for** three hundred yards

**opposite** the bank        **in** bed (in the bed)

I **am** cold. (I have cold.)    I'm hungry.
**Are** you thirsty?

**When** Fred **is** hungry he **goes** to a restaurant.
**When** Lucy **is** thirsty she **has** a drink of water.

He **has** a drink. He **has** a bath. She **has** a wash.

# Words and expressions to learn

## Nouns

the right /ðə 'raɪt/
the left /ðə 'left/
school /sku:l/
home /həʊm/
yard /jɑ:d/

**Learn seven or more of these:**
phone box /'fəʊn bɒks/
supermarket /'su:pəmɑ:kɪt/
bank /bæŋk/
post office /'pəʊst ɒfɪs/
police (plural) /pə'li:s/
police station /pə'li:s steɪʃn/
car park /'kɑ: pɑ:k/
bus stop /'bʌs stɒp/
station /'steɪʃn/
swimming pool /'swɪmɪŋ pu:l/
disco /'dɪskəʊ/
cinema /'sɪnəmə/
the doctor's /ðə 'dɒktəz/
the dentist's /ðə 'dentɪsts/

➡

## Adjectives

**Learn five or more of these:**
hungry /ˈhʌŋgri/
thirsty /ˈθɜːsti/
cold /kəʊld/
hot /hɒt/
nearest /ˈnɪərɪst/
happy /ˈhæpi/
unhappy /ʌnˈhæpi/
bored /bɔːd/
tired /ˈtaɪəd/
wet /wet/
dirty /ˈdɜːti/

## Other words and expressions

there /ðeə(r)/
over there /ˈəʊvə ˈðeə(r)/
then /ðen/
straight on /streɪt ˈɒn/
for three hundred yards
  /fə ˈθriː ˈhʌndrəd ˈjɑːdz/
upstairs /ʌpˈsteəz/
downstairs /daʊnˈsteəz/
near /nɪə(r)/

next to /ˈnekst tə/
opposite /ˈɒpəzɪt/
How far? /haʊ ˈfɑː(r)/
Thank you anyway.
  /θæŋk juː ˈeniweɪ/
Not at all. /nɒt ət ˈɔːl/
at home /ət ˈhəʊm/
at school /ət ˈskuːl/
take /teɪk/

---

# Unit 9

## Grammar and structures

### Complex sentences with conjunctions

These people live in the Amazon Basin, where it is very hot.

I'm sure (that) horses eat grass.
I think (that) penguins live in the Arctic.
I don't think (that) cats eat grass.
~~(I think that cats don't eat grass.)~~

### Word order: position of adverbs

It **often** rains here.
  ~~(It rains often here.)~~
It **never** snows in the Congo.
Cows **certainly** eat grass.

It is **often** cold. ~~(It often is cold.)~~
I am **often** tired.
She is **certainly** right.

**Perhaps** gorillas eat insects.
**Perhaps** you are right.

### *Will*

It often **rains**. It **will rain** tomorrow.
It **is** cold. It **will be** cold tomorrow.
There **is** fog. There **will be** fog tomorrow.

## Words and expressions to learn

### Nouns

day /deɪ/
week /wiːk/
year /jɪə(r)/
spring /sprɪŋ/
summer /ˈsʌmə(r)/
autumn /ˈɔːtəm/
winter /ˈwɪntə(r)/
wood /wʊd/
the rest /ðə ˈrest/

**Learn three or more of these:**
weather /ˈweðə(r)/
rain /reɪn/
sun /sʌn/
sky /skaɪ/
fog /fɒg/
temperature /ˈtemprətʃə(r)/
wind /wɪnd/
cloud /klaʊd/

**Learn two or more of these:**
fish /fɪʃ/
meat /miːt/
fruit /fruːt/
insect /ˈɪnsekt/
vegetable
  /ˈvedʒtəbl/

**Learn two or more of these:**
animal /ˈænɪml/
gorilla /gəˈrɪlə/
camel /ˈkæml/
parrot /ˈpærət/
snake /sneɪk/
polar bear /ˈpəʊlə ˈbeə(r)/
tiger /ˈtaɪgə(r)/
penguin /ˈpeŋgwɪn/
elephant /ˈelɪfənt/

### Verbs

sleep /sliːp/
make /meɪk/
made of /ˈmeɪd əv/
rain /reɪn/
snow /snəʊ/
wear /weə(r)/

### Adjectives

**Learn two or more of these:**
dry /draɪ/
cool /kuːl/
sunny /ˈsʌni/
warm /wɔːm/
cloudy /ˈklaʊdi/
windy /ˈwɪndi/
foggy /ˈfɒgi/
difficult
  /ˈdɪfɪkʊlt/

### Frequency adverbs

never /ˈnevə(r)/
occasionally /əˈkeɪʒnəli/
once every . . . years
  /ˈwʌns ˈevri . . . ˈjɪəz/
sometimes /ˈsʌmtaɪmz/
quite often /ˈkwaɪt ˈɒfn/
often /ˈɒfn/
usually /ˈjuːʒəli/

### Other words and expressions

that (conjunction) /ðət/
few /fjuː/
between /bɪˈtwiːn/
once /wʌns/
tomorrow /təˈmɒrəʊ/
perhaps /pəˈhæps/
certainly /ˈsɜːtənli/
I'm sure /aɪm ˈʃɔː(r)/
on foot /ɒn ˈfʊt/
every /ˈevri/

# Unit 10

## Grammar and structures

### Have got

| | | |
|---|---|---|
| I have got | \| | I've got |
| you have got | \| | you've got |
| he/she/it has got | \| | he's/she's/it's got |
| we have got | \| | we've got |
| you have got | \| | you've got |
| they have got | \| | they've got |

| |
|---|
| have I got? |
| have you got? |
| has he/she/it got? |
| have we got? |
| have you got? |
| have they got? |

| | | |
|---|---|---|
| I have not got | \| | I haven't got |
| you have not got | \| | you haven't got |
| he/she/it has not got | \| | he/she/it hasn't got |
| we have not got | \| | we haven't got |
| you have not got | \| | you haven't got |
| they have not got | \| | they haven't got |

'Have you got any brothers or sisters?'
'Yes, I have.' ~~(Yes, I've.)~~ 'No, I haven't.'

---

## Adjectives

long red hair ~~(red long hair)~~ ~~(hair long red)~~
short grey hair ~~(short and grey hair)~~
a short red dress
*but*: a red **and** white dress

His hair **is** grey. ~~(His hair are grey.)~~
His jeans **are** light blue. ~~(His jeans is...)~~

---

## *Both* and *all*

We are |both / all| fair.     We have |both / all| got fair hair.

We |both / all| live in London.

## Compliments

What **a** pretty dress!     What nice shoes!
**That**'s a nice jacket.   **Those** are nice trousers.

---

What's **this** called in English? What are **these**?

How do you say *boucles d'oreille* in English?

---

What colour **are** her eyes?
Pat **is wearing** blue jeans.

## Words and expressions to learn

### Nouns

photograph (photo) /'fəʊtəgrɑːf ('fəʊtəʊ)/
colour /'kʌlə(r)/

| Learn five or more of these: | |
|---|---|
| eye /aɪ/ | hand /hænd/ |
| nose /nəʊz/ | foot /fʊt/ (*plural* feet /fiːt/) |
| ear /ɪə(r)/ | head /hed/ |
| mouth /maʊθ/ | finger /'fɪŋgə(r)/ |
| face /feɪs/ | beard /bɪəd/ |
| arm /ɑːm/ | moustache /mə'stɑːʃ/ |
| leg /leg/ | tooth /tuːθ/ (*plural* teeth /tiːθ/) |

| Learn five or more of these: | |
|---|---|
| sweater /'swetə(r)/ | blouse /blaʊz/ |
| jacket /'dʒækɪt/ | tights /taɪts/ |
| trousers /'traʊzəz/ | bra /brɑː/ |
| jeans /dʒiːnz/ | pants /pænts/ |
| boots /buːts/ | shirt /ʃɜːt/ |
| shoes /ʃuːz/ | raincoat /'reɪnkəʊt/ |
| socks /sɒks/ | coat /kəʊt/ |
| skirt /skɜːt/ | glasses /'glɑːsɪz/ |
| dress /dres/ | |

### Verbs

touch /tʌtʃ/
arrive at /ə'raɪv ət/
meet /miːt/
say /seɪ/

### Adjectives

| Learn ten or more of these: | |
|---|---|
| long /lɒŋ/ | orange /'ɒrɪndʒ/ |
| short /ʃɔːt/ | yellow /'jeləʊ/ |
| lovely /'lʌvli/ | purple /'pɜːpl/ |
| beautiful /'bjuːtɪfl/ | pink /pɪŋk/ |
| blue /bluː/ | black /blæk/ |
| brown /braʊn/ | white /waɪt/ |
| red /red/ | light /laɪt/ |
| green /griːn/ | dark /dɑːk/ |
| grey /greɪ/ | |

### Other words and expressions

with /wɪð/    lots of /'lɒts əv/
these /ðiːz/    like /laɪk/
those /ðəʊz/    look like /'lʊk laɪk/
all /ɔːl/    personality /pɜːsə'næləti/
except /ɪk'sept/    Dear /dɪə(r)/
more /mɔː(r)/    Yours sincerely /jɔːz sɪn'sɪəli/
a.m. /eɪ 'em/    the others /ðiː 'ʌðəz/
p.m. /piː 'em/    me /miː/

# Unit 12

## Grammar and structures

### Simple Past tense

| | | |
|---|---|---|
| I started<br>you started<br>he/she/it started<br>we started<br>they started | did I start?<br>did you start?<br>did he/she/it start?<br>did we start?<br>did they start? | I did not (didn't) start<br>you did not (didn't) start<br>he/she/it did not (didn't) start<br>we did not (didn't) start<br>they did not (didn't) start |

*Spelling:* work**ed**  listen**ed**  cook**ed**
lived  loved  hated
stop**ped**  shop**ped**  travel**led**
marr**ied**  stud**ied**

*Pronunciation:* -*(e)d* = /d/: died  played  opened  lived  remembered
-*(e)d* = /t/: worked  liked  stopped  danced  watched
-*(e)d* = /ɪd/: started  hated  depended  wanted  assisted

---

### *Was* and *were*

| | | |
|---|---|---|
| I was<br>you were<br>he/she/it was<br>we were<br>they were | was I?<br>were you?<br>was he/she/it?<br>were we?<br>were they? | I was not (wasn't)<br>you were not (weren't)<br>he/she/it was not (wasn't)<br>we were not (weren't)<br>they were not (weren't) |

---

### Pro-verbs

I didn't **like** dancing when I was a boy, but now I **do**.
I **played** chess when I was a child, but now I **don't**.

### *Who*: subject and object

Who wrote to Mary? (~~Who did write to Mary?~~)
Who did Mary write to?

---

### Irregular verbs: Simple Past tense forms

| Infinitive | Simple Past | Infinitive | Simple Past | Infinitive | Simple Past |
|---|---|---|---|---|---|
| be /bi:/ | was, were<br>/wəz, wɒz;<br>wə(r), wɜ:(r)/ | have /həv, hæv/<br>hear /hɪə(r)/<br>know /nəʊ/ | had /həd, hæd/<br>heard /hɜ:d/<br>knew /nju:/ | speak /spi:k/<br>spell /spel/<br>take /teɪk/ | spoke /spəʊk/<br>spelt /spelt/<br>took /tʊk/ |
| become /bɪ'kʌm/<br>can /kən, kæn/<br>come /kʌm/<br>do /du:/<br>drink /drɪŋk/<br>find /faɪnd/<br>get /get/<br>go /gəʊ/ | became /bɪ'keɪm/<br>could /kʊd/<br>came /keɪm/<br>did /dɪd/<br>drank /dræŋk/<br>found /faʊnd/<br>got /gɒt/<br>went /went/ | leave /li:v/<br>make /meɪk/<br>mean /mi:n/<br>meet /mi:t/<br>read /ri:d/<br>say /seɪ/<br>sell /sel/<br>sleep /sli:p/ | left /left/<br>made /meɪd/<br>meant /ment/<br>met /met/<br>read /red/<br>said /sed/<br>sold /səʊld/<br>slept /slept/ | tell /tel/<br>think /θɪŋk/<br>understand<br>  /ʌndə'stænd/<br>wear /weə(r)/<br>write /raɪt/ | told /təʊld/<br>thought /θɔ:t/<br>understood<br>  /ʌndə'stʊd/<br>wore /wɔ:(r)/<br>wrote /rəʊt/ |

## Words and expressions to learn

### Nouns

clerk /klɑ:k/
manager /'mænɪdʒə(r)/
bus driver /'bʌsdraɪvə(r)/
education /edʒə'keɪʃn/
passport /'pɑ:spɔ:t/
paper /'peɪpə(r)/
calculator /'kælkjəleɪtə(r)/
pocket /'pɒkɪt/
midnight /'mɪdnaɪt/

### Verbs

was born, were born /wəz 'bɔ:n, wə 'bɔ:n/
die /daɪ/
marry /'mæri/
leave /li:v/ (*past:* left /left/)
become /bɪ'kʌm/ (*past:* became /bɪ'keɪm/)
tell /tel/ (*past:* told /təʊld/)
come /kʌm/ (*past:* came /keɪm/)
want /wɒnt/
ask /ɑ:sk/
kiss /kɪs/
find /faɪnd/ (*past:* found /faʊnd/)
hear /hɪə(r)/ (*past:* heard /hɜ:d/)
answer /'ɑ:nsə(r)/

## Adjectives

retired /rɪ'taɪəd/
unemployed /ˌʌnɪm'plɔɪd/
late /leɪt/

## Other words and expressions

last night /lɑ:st 'naɪt/
till /tɪl/
a bit /ə 'bɪt/
through /θru:/

when /wen/
actually /'æktʃəli/
again /ə'gen/

# Unit 13

## Grammar and structures

### *This, that, these, those, one(s)*

Could I see **that** watch, please?
**This** one?

No, | **that one.**
| the big **one.**
| the **one** behind the ring.

Could you show me **those** glasses?
**These?**

No, | **those.**
| the red **ones.**
| the **ones** by the teapot.

## Words and expressions to learn

### Nouns

Learn seven or more of these:

thing /θɪŋ/
ring /rɪŋ/
spoon /spu:n/
glass /glɑ:s/
watch /wɒtʃ/
box /bɒks/
size /saɪz/
single /'sɪŋgl/
return /rɪ'tɜ:n/
platform /'plætfɔ:m/
train /treɪn/
meal /mi:l/
cigarette /sɪgə'ret/
hotel /həʊ'tel/

### Verbs

buy /baɪ/ (*past:* bought /bɔ:t/)
take /teɪk/ (*past:* took /tʊk/)
help /help/
look /lʊk/
look for /'lʊk fə(r), 'lʊk fɔ:(r)/
suit /su:t/
fit /fɪt/
try ... on /traɪ ... 'ɒn/
change /tʃeɪndʒ/
see /si:/ (*past:* saw /sɔ:/)
show /ʃəʊ/
would /wʊd/

### Adjectives

larger /'lɑ:dʒə(r)/
next /nekst/
direct /dɪ'rekt/
expensive /ɪks'pensɪv/

### Other words and expressions

one(s) /wʌn(z)/
Here you are. /'hɪə jʊ 'ɑ:/
of course /əv 'kɔ:s/
in front of /ɪn 'frʌnt əv/
behind /bɪ'haɪnd/
other /'ʌðə(r)/
another /ə'nʌðə(r)/ (an other)
really /'rɪəli/
anything /'eniθɪŋ/
I'm afraid... /aɪm ə'freɪd/
just /dʒʌst/
which /wɪtʃ/
Please speak more slowly.
/pli:z 'spi:k mɔ: 'sləʊli/
How do you pronounce...?
/'haʊ də ju: prə'naʊns/
Is this correct...? /ɪz 'ðɪs kə'rekt/
without /wɪ'ðaʊt/
OK /əʊ 'keɪ/

# Unit 14

## Grammar and structures

### *Can*

| I can<br>you can<br>he/she/it can<br>we can<br>they can | can I?<br>can you?<br>can he/she/it?<br>can we?<br>can they?<br><br>(do you can?) | I cannot (can't)<br>you cannot (can't)<br>he/she/it cannot (can't)<br>we cannot (can't)<br>they cannot (can't) |

*Pronunciation:* /kn/: I can swim.
/kn/ or /kæn/:
    Can you play tennis?
/kæn/: Yes, I can.
/kɑ:nt/:
    No, I can't. I can't play tennis.

➡

## Adjectives

*Comparatives and superlatives:*

old / older / oldest; cheap / cheaper / cheapest
fat / fatter / fattest
happy / happier / happiest
fine / finer / finest
interesting / **more** interesting / **most** interesting
good / **better** / **best**
bad / **worse** / **worst**

I'm tall**er than** (/ðən/) my brother.
I'm **much** tall**er than** my mother.
I'm **a bit** tall**er than** my sister.
I'm **the** tall**est** person **in** my family.

## Comparing

I can cook **better** / run fast**er** / sing high**er than** my brother.
I can ski **better** now **than** I could when I was younger.

I was **good at** maths / swimming when I was younger, but I'm not now.

Peking is **the same as** Beijing.
A typist is **not the same as** a typewriter.
A café is **different from** (/frəm/) a pub.

I'm **as** (/əz/) strong **as** (/əz/) my husband.
A Rolls-Royce is **not as** noisy **as** a Volkswagen.

# Words and expressions to learn

## Nouns

chess /tʃes/
typewriter /'taɪpraɪtə(r)/
typist /'taɪpɪst/

## Verbs

run /rʌn/ (*past:* ran /ræn/)
ski /ski:/
sing /sɪŋ/ (*past:* sang /sæŋ/)
go without sleep
type /taɪp/
drive /draɪv/ (*past:* drove /drəʊv/)
draw /drɔ:/ (*past:* drew /dru:/)
swim /swɪm/ (*past:* swam /swæm/)
count /kaʊnt/

## Adjectives

better /'betə(r)/ best /best/
fast /fɑ:st/
cheap /tʃi:p/
easy /'i:zi/
bad /bæd/ worse /wɜ:s/
  worst /wɜ:st/
comfortable /'kʌmftəbl/
economical /ekə'nɒmɪkl/
rich /rɪtʃ/
funny /'fʌni/
interesting /'ɪntrəstɪŋ/
handsome /'hænsəm/
heavy /'hevi/

## Adverbs

better /'betə(r)/
fast /fɑ:st/
faster /'fɑ:stə(r)/
cheaper /'tʃi:pə(r)/
now /naʊ/
well /wel/

## Other words and expressions

the same /ðə 'seɪm/
as /əz, æz/
than /ðən, ðæn/

---

# Unit 15

## Grammar and structures

### *Ago*

'How long ago (/'haʊ 'lɒŋ ə'gəʊ/) did the last dinosaurs die?'
  'About 70 million years ago.' (/'jɪəzə'gəʊ/)
Julius Caesar invaded Britain about 2,000 years ago.
'How long ago was Galileo born?' 'About 400 years ago.'

ten years ago      a year ago      two months ago
a week ago      two days ago      a minute ago

### Time sequences

On the night of . . . , . . .
As soon as . . . , . . .
Then . . .
After . . . , . . .
And then . . .
Finally, . . .

## Words and expressions to learn

### Nouns

Africa /'æfrɪkə/
Asia /'eɪʃə/
Europe /'jʊərəp/

Australia /ɒ'streɪljə/
America /ə'merɪkə/
part /pɑ:t/

university /ju:nɪ'vɜ:sɪti/
plane /pleɪn/
republic /rɪ'pʌblɪk/

world /wɜ:ld/
radio /'reɪdɪəʊ/
novel /'nɒvl/

146

## Verbs

begin /bɪ'gɪn/ (*past:* began /bɪ'gæn/)
move /mu:v/
separate /'sepəreɪt/
finish /'fɪnɪʃ/
lose /lu:z/ (*past:* lost /lɒst/)
laugh /lɑ:f/
take (a person to a place) /teɪk/
decide /dɪ'saɪd/
disagree /dɪsə'gri:/
discover /dɪs'kʌvə(r)/
walk /wɔ:k/
break (into) /'breɪk ('ɪntə)/(*past:* broke /brəʊk/)
wake (up) /'weɪk ('ʌp)/ (*past:* woke /'weʊk/)
kill /kɪl/
build /bɪld/ (*past:* built /bɪlt/)

## Other words and expressions

ago /ə'gəʊ/
still /stɪl/
across /ə'krɒs/
finally /'faɪnəli/
as soon as /əz 'su:n əz/
on the night of /ɒn ðə 'naɪt əv/
some of /'sʌm əv/
slow /sləʊ/
a long time /ə 'lɒŋ taɪm/
last /lɑ:st/
back /bæk/

# Unit 16

## Grammar and structures

### Ages, heights, weights

Our house **is** four hundred years old.
The baby **is** six months old.
John **is** thirty-two (years old).
(John is thirty-two years.)

I **am** six feet tall.
My mother **is** five feet six (inches tall).
5ft 6ins.
I **weigh** 180 pounds (lbs).

### Be like / look like

'What **is** your sister **like**?' 'She's very shy.
She likes cycling and modern dance.'
'What **does** your sister **look like**?' 'She's
tall and dark. She's quite pretty.'

He **looks** bad-tempered.
He **looks like** a scientist.

### Dates

Jan 14, 1978. January the fourteenth,
nineteen seventy-eight.

My birthday is on January the fourteenth.

### A and *any*

I haven't got **any** money.
I haven't got **any** cigarettes.
I haven't got **a** car.
(I haven't got any car.)

## Words and expressions to learn

### Nouns

building /'bɪldɪŋ/
foot /fʊt/ (*plural* feet /fi:t/)
inch /ɪntʃ/
pound /paʊnd/
height /haɪt/
weight /weɪt/
month /mʌnθ/
birthday /'bɜ:θdeɪ/
date /deɪt/
bicycle /'baɪsɪkl/
guitar /gɪ'tɑ:(r)/
businessman /'bɪznɪsmən/
scientist /'saɪəntɪst/
politician /pɒlɪ'tɪʃn/

### Adjectives

**Learn five or more of these:**
new /nju:/
kind /kaɪnd/
shy /ʃaɪ/
sensitive /'sensətɪv/
self-confident /self'kɒnfɪdənt/
stupid /'stju:pɪd/
bad-tempered /bæd 'tempəd/
calm /kɑ:m/
friendly /'frendli/
nervy /'nɜ:vi/

### The months

January /'dʒænjəri/
February /'febrəri/
March /mɑ:tʃ/
April /'eɪprʊl/
May /meɪ/
June /dʒu:n/
July /dʒu:'laɪ/
August /'ɔ:gəst/
September /sep'tembə(r)/
October /ɒk'təʊbə(r)/
November /nəʊ'vembə(r)/
December /dɪ'sembə(r)/

### Numbers

10th   tenth /tenθ/
11th   eleventh /ɪ'levənθ/
12th   twelfth /twelfθ/
13th   thirteenth /θɜ:'ti:nθ/
20th   twentieth /'twentɪəθ/
21st   twenty-first /twenti'fɜ:st/
22nd   twenty-second
　　　 /twenti'sekənd/
25th   twenty-fifth /twenti'fɪfθ/
30th   thirtieth /'θɜ:tɪəθ/
40th   fortieth /'fɔ:tɪəθ/
50th   fiftieth /'fɪftɪəθ/
100th  hundredth /'hʌndrədθ/

### Other words and expressions

weigh /weɪ/
today /tə'deɪ/
I don't agree. /aɪ dəʊnt ə'gri:/
Happy birthday. /hæpi 'bɜ:θdeɪ/

# Unit 17

## Grammar and structures

### Requests and answers

I'll have a rump steak.    I'll start with soup.

| Could you | bring me the bill? | Yes, of course. |
|---|---|---|
| | give us some more coffee? | I'm sorry, I need it/them. |
| | show me some sweaters? | I'm afraid I can't. |
| | lend me a pen? | I haven't got one. |
| | lend me your keys? | I haven't got any. |

Could you possibly lend me . . . ?
Can I talk to you for a minute? (Can I talk you . . . ?)

### Quantities

a little water (a little of water) (a few water)
a few biscuits (a few of biscuits)
no more roast beef (no more of roast beef)
a piece of bread
a cup of coffee

Would you like **something** to eat?
I don't want **anything** to eat, thank you.
**nothing** to drink

### Personal pronouns and possessives

| SUBJECT | OBJECT | POSSESSIVE |
|---|---|---|
| I | me | my |
| you | you | your |
| he | him | his |
| she | her | her |
| it | it | its |
| we | us | our |
| you | you | your |
| they | them | their |

(For examples, see Lesson 17D.)

## Words and expressions to learn

### Nouns

bill /bɪl/
hour /'aʊə(r)/
half an hour
　/hɑːf ən 'aʊə(r)/
minute /'mɪnɪt/
surprise /sə'praɪz/

piece /piːs/
cup /kʌp/
restaurant
　/'restrənt/

**Learn two or more of these:**
beef /biːf/          apple /'æpl/
chicken /'tʃɪkɪn/    biscuit
salad /'sæləd/          /'bɪskɪt/
steak /steɪk/
mushroom /'mʌʃruːm/
sugar /'ʃʊgə(r)/

**Learn two or more of these:**
dictionary /'dɪkʃənri/
lighter /'laɪtə(r)/
key /kiː/
umbrella /ʌm'brelə/
pen /pen/
pencil /'pensl/

### Verbs

bring /brɪŋ/
　(past: brought /brɔːt/)
give /gɪv/ (past: gave /geɪv/)
lend /lend/ (past: lent /lent/)
borrow /'bɒrəʊ/
need /niːd/
talk /tɔːk/
smoke /sməʊk/
eat /iːt/ (past: ate /et/)
I'll (I will) /aɪl (aɪ 'wɪl)/

### Adjectives

polite /pə'laɪt/
rude /ruːd/
all right /ɔːl 'raɪt/
not too bad /nɒt tuː 'bæd/

### Other words and expressions

something /'sʌmθɪŋ/
everything /'evriθɪŋ/
nothing /'nʌθɪŋ/
us /əs, ʌs/
for /fə(r), fɔː(r)/
Come in. /kʌm 'ɪn/
a few /ə 'fjuː/
Is service included? /ɪz 'sɜːvɪs ɪn'kluːdɪd/
Sorry to trouble you. /'sɒri tə 'trʌbl juː/
Have you got a light? /'hæv juː 'gɒt ə 'laɪt/
Just a minute. /'dʒʌst ə 'mɪnɪt/
Help yourself to . . . /'help jɔː'self tə/
I don't smoke. /aɪ 'dəʊnt 'sməʊk/

# Unit 18

## Grammar and structures

### Present Progressive tense

| | | |
|---|---|---|
| I am (I'm) going<br>you are (you're) going<br>he/she/it is ('s) going<br>we are (we're) going<br>they are (they're) going | am I going?<br>are you going?<br>is he/she/it going?<br>are we going?<br>are they going? | I am (I'm) not going<br>you are not (aren't) going<br>he/she/it is not (isn't) going<br>we are not (aren't) going<br>they are not (aren't) going |

**I'm working** very hard just now. (I work . . .)   **I work** on Saturdays. (I'm working . . .)

The price of oil **is going** up. '**Is** your English **getting** better?' 'Yes, it is.' (Yes, it's.)
What**'s** the woman in blue **talking** about? What**'s happening**?

### Spelling

| | | | | |
|---|---|---|---|---|
| start start**ing** | look look**ing** | ma**ke** ma**king** | sto**p** sto**pping** | lie l**ying** |
| speak speak**ing** | play play**ing** | wri**te** wri**ting** | si**t** si**tting** | die d**ying** |
| lend lend**ing** | | | | |

## Words and expressions to learn

### Nouns

postcard /'pəʊstkɑ:d/
bar /bɑ:(r)/
café /'kæfeɪ/
post /pəʊst/
problem /'prɒbləm/
length /leŋkθ/

### Verbs

stand /stænd/ (*past:* stood /stʊd/)
sit /sɪt/ (*past:* sat /sæt/)
lie /laɪ/ (*past:* lay /leɪ/)
fight /faɪt/ (*past:* fought /fɔ:t/)
happen /'hæpn/

send /send/ (*past:* sent /sent/)
look at /'lʊk ət/
have a bath /'hæv ə 'bɑ:θ/
go up /gəʊ 'ʌp/
go down /gəʊ 'daʊn/
fall /fɔ:l/ (*past:* fell /fel/)
rise /raɪz/ (*past:* rose /rəʊz/)
change /tʃeɪndʒ/
get /get/ (*past:* got /gɒt/)
spend /spend/ (*past:* spent /spent/)
stay /steɪ/
wash /wɒʃ/
clean /kli:n/

### Adjectives

wonderful /'wʌndəfl/
boring /'bɔ:rɪŋ/
average /'ævərɪdʒ/

### Other words and expressions

out of /'aʊt əv/
on the phone /ɒn ðə 'fəʊn/
probably /'prɒbəbli/
up /ʌp/
down /daʊn/
under /'ʌndə(r)/

# Unit 19

## Grammar and structures

### Future

**I'm playing** football next weekend.
What **are you doing** this evening?

### Prepositions of time

**on** Tuesday   **on** Tuesday morning   **on** my birthday
**at** the weekend   **at** Christmas   **at** ten o'clock
**in** the morning   **in** the afternoon   **in** the evening
My train leaves **in** half an hour.

*No prepositions with:* today, tomorrow, yesterday,
this, next, last.

She's leaving **tomorrow**. I'm seeing him **next** Tuesday.

### Suggestions

**Let's go** to Spain. **Let's have** a party.
**Why don't we go** to Spain? **Why don't we have** a party?

### Distances

How far **is** Oxford from London?
Oxford **is** 60 miles from London.

### So

Manchester are not playing Liverpool or Tottenham.
**So** Manchester are playing Arsenal.

I'm tired, **so** I'm going to bed.
She felt hungry, **so** she cooked herself an omelette.

## Words and expressions to learn

### Nouns

football /'fʊtbɔ:l/
ticket /'tɪkɪt/
traveller's cheque /'trævləz 'tʃek/
office /'ɒfɪs/
suggestion /sə'dʒestʃən/
conversation /kɒnvə'seɪʃn/
visit /'vɪzɪt/
pub /pʌb/
idea /aɪ'dɪə/
cheque /tʃek/

### Verbs

get (= 'obtain') /get/
forget /fə'get/ (past: forgot /fə'gɒt/)

### Adjectives

excited /ɪk'saɪtɪd/
usual /'ju:ʒʊəl/
impatient /ɪm'peɪʃənt/
free /fri:/

### Other words and expressions

each /i:tʃ/
somebody /'sʌmbədi/
against /ə'genst/
so /səʊ/
Let's /lets/
why /waɪ/
Why don't we...?
I don't want to.
this morning
this afternoon
this evening
I'd love to.
How about...?
I think so.
do the packing /du: ðə 'pækɪŋ/
I hope /aɪ 'həʊp/
catch a plane, train etc. /kætʃ ə 'pleɪn/
have a drink /'hæv ə 'drɪŋk/
a long way /ə lɒŋ 'weɪ/

Summary

# Unit 20

## Grammar and structures

### Present Perfect tense: forms

| I have (I've) | been |
|---|---|
| you have (you've) | lived |
| he/she/it has ('s) | known |
| etc. | had |
| | etc. |

| have I | been? |
|---|---|
| etc. | lived? |
| | known? |
| | had? |
| | etc. |

| I have not (haven't) | been |
|---|---|
| etc. | lived |
| | known |
| | had |
| | etc. |

### Present Perfect tense: use

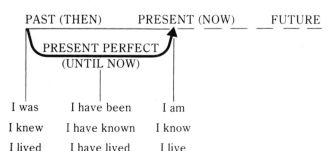

PAST (THEN)      PRESENT (NOW)      FUTURE

PRESENT PERFECT
(UNTIL NOW)

| I was | I have been | I am |
| I knew | I have known | I know |
| I lived | I have lived | I live |

**I have been** here for half an hour. (I am here for...)
**I've known** her since 1948. (I know her...)
How long **have you lived** in England?
How long **have you been** learning English?
**Have you ever been** to Africa?
**Have you read** *War and Peace?*
**Have you seen** *Love Story?*

## Infinitives, past tenses and past participles

*Infinitive*
Would you like **to live** in Scotland?
I want **to go** home.
Let's **have** a party.
Does your mother **know** Alice and John?

*Past tenses*
We **lived** in Ireland when I was a child.
I **went** to bed at twelve.
We **had** a great party on Saturday.
I **knew** him at university.

*Past participles*
I've never **lived** in a flat.
Have you **been** to Africa?
I've always **had** lots of friends.
I've **known** her for twelve years.

| INFINITIVE | PAST TENSE | PAST PARTICIPLE |
|---|---|---|
| *Regular verbs* | | |
| live | lived | lived |
| work | worked | worked |
| stay | stayed | stayed |
| borrow | borrowed | borrowed |
| *Irregular verbs* | | |
| be | was, were | been |
| go | went | gone, been |
| have | had | had |
| know | knew | known |
| see | saw | seen |
| hear | heard | heard |
| read (/riːd/) | read (/red/) | read (/red/) |
| write | wrote | written |

## Since and *for*

I've known him **since** he was a baby.
I've known him **since** 1948.
I've known him **for** nearly 40 years.
I've known him **for** a long time.

## Word order

I **never** eat fish.
I **hardly ever** go to restaurants.
I **sometimes** eat beef.
I **very often** eat lamb.
I **always** drink wine.

I go to London **every Wednesday**.
I go on holiday **twice a year**.
I go to the hairdresser **every two weeks**.

## Reply questions

'I'm tired'. '**Are you?**'
'It's late.' '**Is it?**'
'I love skiing.' '**Do you?**'
'I can't understand her.' '**Can't you?**'
'She's got a new boyfriend.' '**Has she?**'

## So am I, etc.

'I'm tired.' '**So am I.**'
'I've got a cold.' '**So have I.**'
'I can speak Italian.' '**So can I.**'
'I like her very much.' '**So do I.**'

## Requests and answers

'Do you mind if I open a window?' 'Not at all. Please do.'

'Do you mind if I smoke?' 'I'd rather you didn't.'

# Words and expressions to learn

## Nouns

seat /siːt/
paper (= 'newspaper') /'peɪpə(r)/
record /'rekɔːd/
hairdresser /'heədresə(r)/
walk /wɔːk/
pint /paɪnt/
life /laɪf/ (*plural* lives /laɪvz/)

## Verbs

mind /maɪnd/
believe /bɪ'liːv/
learn /lɜːn/ (learnt /lɜːnt/, learnt /lɜːnt/)
must /məst, mʌst/

## Adverbs

always /'ɔːlwɪz/
hardly ever /hɑːdli 'evə(r)/
ever /'evə(r)/
twice /twaɪs/
three times /'θriː 'taɪmz/
already /ɔːl'redi/
so /səʊ/
tonight /tə'naɪt/

## Other words and expressions

if /ɪf/
Please do.
go ahead /gəʊ ə'hed/
favourite /'feɪvrɪt/
great /greɪt/
for (time) /fə(r), fɔː(r)/
for a moment /fər ə 'məʊmənt/
since /sɪns/
go to the cinema
go for a walk
cheers /tʃɪəz/
Have another drink.
all my life
and so on
in love
I feel /aɪ 'fiːl/
myself /maɪ'self/
I'd rather /aɪd 'rɑːðə(r)/

# Unit 21

## Grammar and structures

### Passives

| Cheese<br>Wine<br>Perfume | is | made<br>produced | in | Italy.<br>France. |
|---|---|---|---|---|

| Cameras<br>Cars<br>Calculators | are | made<br>produced<br>manufactured | in | the USA.<br>Japan. |
|---|---|---|---|---|

Where **are** Volvos **manufactured**?   Where **is** Coca Cola **made**?

| Where **were** your | shoes<br>glasses | made? |
|---|---|---|

| Where **was** your | car<br>camera | made? |
|---|---|---|

### Reasons

**Why** can't you throw a fridge?
**Because** it's **too** heavy.
**Because** I'm **not** strong **enough**. (~~enough strong~~)

## Words and expressions to learn

### Nouns

Learn fifteen or more of these:
wool /wʊl/
china /'tʃaɪnə/
leather /'leðə(r)/
metal /'metl/
stone /stəʊn/
rubber /'rʌbə(r)/
plastic /'plæstɪk/
chocolate /'tʃɒklət/
rice /raɪs/
butter /'bʌtə(r)/
skin /skɪn/
business /'bɪznɪs/
chemical /'kemɪkl/
clock /klɒk/
camera /'kæmrə/
knife /naɪf/
   (*plural* knives /naɪvz/)
bird /bɜ:d/
import /'ɪmpɔ:t/
export /'ekspɔ:t/
machine /mə'ʃi:n/
region /'ri:dʒən/

### Verbs

Learn six or more of these:
break /breɪk/ (broke /brəʊk/,
   broken /'brəʊkn/)
break down /breɪk 'daʊn/
use /ju:z/
export /ɪks'pɔ:t/
import /ɪm'pɔ:t/
cost /kɒst/ (cost, cost)
produce /prə'dju:s/
manufacture /mænjʊ'fæktʃə(r)/
boil /bɔɪl/
jump /dʒʌmp/
sunbathe /'sʌnbeɪð/

### Adjectives

Learn six or more of these:
hard /hɑ:d/
tough /tʌf/
light /laɪt/
wide /waɪd/
high /haɪ/
loud /laʊd/
narrow /'nærəʊ/
low /ləʊ/
useful /'ju:sfl/
liquid /'lɪkwɪd/
perfect /'pɜ:fɪkt/

### Other words and expressions

Learn four or more of these:
because /bɪ'kɒz/
together /tə'geðə(r)/
too /tu:/
carefully /'keəfli/
mainly /'meɪnli/
mostly /'məʊstli/

# Unit 23

## Grammar and structures

### Imperatives

**Wear** comfortable clothing.
Always **warm up**.
Never **run** in fog.
**Don't run** after a meal.

**Don't run** if you have a cold.

### Prepositions of position and movement

*Position:* on, in, under, by
*Movement:* on, on to, in, into, under, by, off, out of

### Instructions

*Written instructions:* Wash mushrooms and pat dry.
*Spoken instructions:* **You** wash **the** mushrooms and pat **them** dry.

It's on the chair. It **should be** on the table.

## Words and expressions to learn

### Nouns

advice /əd'vaɪs/ (uncountable)
a cold /ə 'kəʊld/
picture /'pɪktʃə(r)/
floor /flɔ:(r)/

**Learn six or more of these:**
lemon /'lemən/
pepper /'pepə(r)/
salt /sɔ:lt/
juice /dʒu:s/
fork /fɔ:k/
tablespoon /'teɪblspu:n/
bowl /bəʊl/
oil /ɔɪl/
cloth /klɒθ/
frying pan /'fraɪɪŋ 'pæn/
saucepan /'sɔ:spən/

### Verbs

hurry /'hʌri/ (hurried, hurried)
worry /'wʌri/ (worried, worried)
wait /weɪt/
follow /'fɒləʊ/
drop /drɒp/ (dropped, dropped)
pick up /pɪk 'ʌp/
throw /θrəʊ/ (threw /θru:/,
   thrown /θrəʊn/)
throw away /θrəʊ ə'weɪ/
put away /pʊt ə'weɪ/
rest /rest/
should /ʃʊd/

**Learn one or more of these:**
fry /fraɪ/
slice /slaɪs/
mix /mɪks/
pour /pɔ:(r)/

### Other words and expressions

before /bɪ'fɔ:(r)/
into /'ɪntə/
off /ɒf/
fresh /freʃ/
alone /ə'ləʊn/
most of /'məʊst əv/
early /'ɜ:li/
away /ə'weɪ/
after (conjunction) /'ɑ:ftə(r)/
Look out. /lʊk 'aʊt/
Be careful. /bi 'keəfl/
take (your) time /'teɪk (jə) 'taɪm/

# Unit 24

## Grammar and structures

| a dollar | | night |
|----------|---|-------|
| 57 pence | **a** | kilo |
| an apple | | day |

To get from Oxford Circus to Paddington, you **have to** change twice.

You can get from Bond Street to Leicester Square **without changing**.

➡

## Words and expressions to learn

### Nouns

credit card /'kredɪt kɑːd/
cash /kæʃ/
shower /ʃaʊə(r)/
form /fɔːm/
stop /stɒp/
line /laɪn/
way /weɪ/
boarding pass /'bɔːdɪŋ pɑːs/
gate /geɪt/
flight /flaɪt/
arrival /ə'raɪvl/
departure /dɪ'pɑːtʃə/
reservation /rezə'veɪʃn/
hand baggage /'hænd 'bægɪdʒ/
timetable /'taɪmteɪbl/
air /eə(r)/
airport /'eəpɔːt/

airline /'eəlaɪn/
side /saɪd/
crossroads /'krɒsrəʊdz/
bridge /brɪdʒ/
river /'rɪvə(r)/

### Verbs

get to /'get tə, 'get tuː/
pay /peɪ/ (paid /peɪd/, paid /peɪd/)
check in /tʃek 'ɪn/
fill in /fɪl 'ɪn/
have to /'hæftə, 'hæftuː/

### Other words and expressions

including /ɪŋ'kluːdɪŋ/
over /'əʊvə(r)/
along /ə'lɒŋ/
on to /'ɒntə, 'ɒntʊ/
by credit card
by cheque
in cash
on the way
by air
double room /'dʌbl 'ruːm/

---

# Unit 25

## Grammar and structures

### *Going to*

I'm **going to write** letters this evening.
This is **going to be** my room.
She's **going to have** a baby.
What are all your friends **going to do** when they leave school?

---

'Why did you come here?' '**To see** you.' ~~(For to see you.)~~

---

### Infinitives and -*ing* forms

*Infinitive without to*: I can **swim**.
*Infinitive with to*: Would you like **to dance**?
-*ing form*: Do you like **dancing**?
(For details, see Lesson 25D.)

---

## Words and expressions to learn

### Nouns

plan /plæn/
country /'kʌntri/
cost /kɒst/
details /'diːteɪlz/
library /'laɪbri/
butcher's /'bʊtʃəz/
embassy /'embəsi/
travel agent /'trævl 'eɪdʒənt/
information /ɪnfə'meɪʃn/
visa /'viːzə/
suitcase /'suːtkeɪs/
aeroplane /'eərəpleɪn/
air ticket /'eə tɪkɪt/
baby /'beɪbi/

### Verbs

study /'stʌdi/
win /wɪn/ (won /wʌn/, won /wʌn/)
crash /kræʃ/
organize /'ɔːgənaɪz/
join /dʒɔɪn/

### Other words and expressions

fit /fɪt/
inclusive /ɪŋ'kluːsɪv/
hard work /'hɑːd 'wɜːk/
have a baby /'hæv ə 'beɪbi/
first of all /'fɜːst əv 'ɔːl/
not yet /nɒt 'jet/
play cards /pleɪ 'kɑːdz/

154

# Unit 26

## Grammar and structures

### Feelings

| It | depresses<br>frightens | me. | | It makes me | angry.<br>happy.<br>unhappy. | | He gets | angry<br>worried<br>bored | when he goes there. |

### *-ed* and *-ing*

Does this **interest** you? It **interests** me. I'm **interested** in it. It's **interesting**. (I'm interesting in it.)
Does John **bore** you? He **bores** me. I'm **bored**. He's **boring**. (I'm boring by him.)

| easy<br>nice<br>difficult | to | talk **to**<br>work **with**<br>see | etc. |

## Words and expressions to learn

### Nouns

flu /fluː/ (uncountable)
a temperature /ə ˈtemprɪtʃə(r)/
  (countable)
headache /ˈhedeɪk/ (countable)
toothache /ˈtuːθeɪk/ (uncountable)
aspirin /ˈæsprɪn/
medicine /ˈmedsən/
matter /ˈmætə(r)/
dinner /ˈdɪnə(r)/
pleasure /ˈpleʒə(r)/
freedom /ˈfriːdəm/
mistake /mɪsˈteɪk/
marriage /ˈmærɪdʒ/
couple /ˈkʌpl/

### Verbs

feel /fiːl/ (felt /felt/, felt /felt/)
hurt /hɜːt/ (hurt /hɜːt/, hurt /hɜːt/)
frighten /ˈfraɪtn/
depress /dɪˈpres/
disgust /dɪsˈɡʌst/
solve /sɒlv/
trust /trʌst/
get on (with) /get ˈɒn (wɪð)/
can't stand /kɑːnt ˈstænd/
appreciate /əˈpriːʃieɪt/
share /ʃeə(r)/
lie down /laɪ ˈdaʊn/
  (lay /leɪ/, lain /leɪn/)

### Adjectives

ill /ɪl/
angry /ˈæŋɡri/
fed up /ˈfed ˈʌp/
fair /feə(r)/

### Other words and expressions

That's very nice of you.
on the whole /ɒn ðə ˈhəʊl/
take medicine /ˈteɪk ˈmedsən/
What's the matter?
change (my) mind
  /ˈtʃeɪndʒ (maɪ) ˈmaɪnd/

# Unit 27

## Grammar and structures

### *Get*

**Get** + **noun** = *receive, obtain, fetch* etc.
  *get a letter   get a drink*

**Get** + **adverb particle/preposition** = *move*
  *get up   get into a car*

**Get** + **adjective** = *become*
  *It's getting cold.*

### *Have got*
  *I've got two brothers.*

### Adverbs of manner

She speaks English **well**. (She speaks well English.)
I like skiing **very much**. (I like very much skiing.)

slow – slow**ly**
careful – careful**ly**
nice – nice**ly**

happy – happ**ily**
comfortable – comforta**bly**

➡

155

## Words and expressions to learn

### Nouns

boat /bəʊt/
motorbike /'məʊtəbaɪk/
taxi /'tæksi/
bus /bʌs/
journey /'dʒɜ:ni/
lightning /'laɪtnɪŋ/
race /reɪs/
speed /spi:d/
record /'rekɔ:d/
button /'bʌtn/
handle /'hændl/
packet /'pækɪt/
flower /'flaʊə(r)/
second /'sekənd/

### Verbs

ride /raɪd/ (rode /rəʊd/,
  ridden /'rɪdn/)
fly /flaɪ/ (flew /flu:/, flown /fləʊn/)
hitchhike /'hɪtʃhaɪk/
guess /ges/
press /pres/
pull /pʊl/
push /pʊʃ/
turn /tɜ:n/
get on /get ɒn/
get off /get ɒf/
get in(to) /get 'ɪn(tə)/
get out (of) /get 'aʊt (əv)/
breathe /bri:ð/

### Adjectives

electric /ɪ'lektrɪk/
sleepy /'sli:pi/
thin /θɪn/

### Adverbs

sleepily /'sli:pəli/
happily /'hæpəli/
kindly /'kaɪndli/
angrily /'æŋgrəli/
loudly /'laʊdli/
quietly /'kwaɪətli/
coldly /'kəʊldli/
shyly /'ʃaɪli/
noisily /'nɔɪzəli/
badly /'bædli/
nicely /'naɪsli/
comfortably /'kʌmftəbli/

### Other words and expressions

by plane /baɪ 'pleɪn/
by boat /baɪ 'bəʊt/
one day /wʌn 'deɪ/
like lightning /laɪk 'laɪtnɪŋ/

---

# Unit 28

## Grammar and structures

### Quantifiers

Very few pupils go to private schools.
Not many pupils...
Some pupils...
Two thirds of American pupils...
Three quarters of...
Most pupils...
Nearly all pupils...
More British pupils... than American pupils...
Far more pupils...
75% of American pupils...
Less than 5% of British pupils...

### Fractions

⅔ two thirds
¾ three quarters
⅞ seven eighths
³⁄₂₀ three twentieths

### Prepositions

**at** the top    **at** the bottom
**at** the beginning    **at** the end
**in** the middle
**at** 16 (years old)

### Structuring paragraphs

First...   Next...   Then...   After that...   Finally...

---

## Words and expressions to learn

### Nouns

private school /'praɪvɪt 'sku:l/
state school /'steɪt 'sku:l/
country /'kʌntri/
top /tɒp/
bottom /'bɒtəm/
front /frʌnt/
back /bæk/
corner /'kɔ:nə(r)/
middle /'mɪdl/
circle /'sɜ:kl/

cross /krɒs/
square /skweə(r)/
triangle /'traɪæŋgl/
beginning /bɪ'gɪnɪŋ/
end /end/
soup /su:p/
theatre /'θɪətə(r)/
zoo /zu:/
policeman /pə'li:smən/
map /mæp/

156

## Verbs

shave /ʃeɪv/
wash /wɒʃ/
get dressed /get 'drest/
put on (clothes) /pʊt 'ɒn/
take off (clothes) /teɪk 'ɒf/
brush (teeth, hair) /brʌʃ/
go out (lights etc.) /gəʊ 'aʊt/
ring (phone) /rɪŋ/ (rang/ræŋ/, rung/rʌŋ/)

## Other words and expressions

far more /'fɑː 'mɔː(r)/
most /məʊst/
less /les/
nearly /'nɪəli/
true /truː/
inside /in'saɪd/
outside /aʊt'saɪd/
What else? /wɒt 'els/

# Unit 29

## Grammar and structures

**Future: *will***

| | | |
|---|---|---|
| I will start | ǀ | I'll start |
| you will start | ǀ | you'll start |
| he/she/it will start | ǀ | he'll/she'll/it'll start |
| we will start | ǀ | we'll start |
| they will start | ǀ | they'll start |

| | | | |
|---|---|---|---|
| will I start? | I will not start | ǀ | I won't start |
| will you start? | you will not start | ǀ | you won't start |
| etc. | etc. | ǀ | etc. |

**I'll** take money with me.
**You'll** get lost. No, I **won't**.
You **won't** get lifts. Yes, I **will**.

### *Get*

You'll **get** lost. You'll **get** killed.
I'm going to **get** married.

## Words and expressions to learn

### Nouns

**Learn six or more of these:**
word /wɜːd/
death /deθ/
heart /hɑːt/
lover /'lʌvə(r)/
youth hostel /'juːθ hɒstl/
prison /'prɪzn/
pilot /'paɪlət/
decision /dɪ'sɪʒən/
trouble /'trʌbl/
accident /'æksɪdənt/
opportunity /ɒpə'tjuːnəti/
news /njuːz/
star /stɑː(r)/
misunderstanding
  /mɪsʌndə'stændɪŋ/

**Learn six or more of these:**
tractor /'træktə(r)/
rope /rəʊp/
bottle /'bɒtl/
blanket /'blæŋkɪt/
tent /tent/
gas /gæs/
sunglasses /'sʌnglɑːsɪz/
matches /'mætʃɪz/
tin /tɪn/
tin-opener /'tɪn'əʊpnə(r)/
toothbrush /'tuːθbrʌʃ/
rifle /'raɪfl/
compass /'kʌmpəs/
backpack /'bækpæk/

### Verbs

get lost /get 'lɒst/
get married /get 'mærɪd/
enjoy /in'dʒɔɪ/
won't /wəʊnt/
dream /driːm/
pass /pɑːs/
fall in love /fɔːl in 'lʌv/

### Adjectives

dangerous /'deɪndʒərəs/
dead /ded/
tinned /tɪnd/
famous /'feɪməs/

### Preposition

round /raʊnd/

# Unit 30

## Grammar and structures

### Use

A farmer uses a barn to keep cows in.     A farmer keeps cows in a barn.
Nurses use thermometers to take temperatures with.     Nurses take temperatures with thermometers.
You use a wallet to keep money in.     You keep money in a wallet.
You use a key to open a door with.     You open a door with a key.

### Stress

'You've got *two* sisters, haven't you?' 'No, just one.'
'You've got two *sisters*, haven't you?' 'No, two brothers.'

### Words having different functions

| *Verb* | *Noun* | *Adjective* |
|---|---|---|
| 1. **Phone** me at 7.00. | 1. a blue **phone** | 1. – |
| 2. Could you **bath** the baby? | 2. He's having a **bath**. | 2. – |
| 3. **Open** your mouth and say 'Ah'. | 3. – | 3. The door was partly **open**. |
| 4. It doesn't **dry** my hair. | 4. – | 4. It was a very **dry** day. |
| 5. – | 5. Have an **orange**. | 5. an **orange** car |

### Nouns used a little like adjectives

a **box** with a **phone** in it = a **phone box**
a **shop** that sells **books** = a **book shop** (a books shop)
a **wheel** of a **bicycle** = a **bicycle wheel**
a **race** for **horses** = a **horse race**

## Words and expressions to learn

### Nouns

garden /'gɑ:dn/
petrol /'petrʊl/
oil /ɔɪl/
complaint /kəm'pleɪnt/
appointment /ə'pɔɪntmənt/
customer /'kʌstəmə(r)/

**Learn six or more of these:**
mathematics /mæθ'mætɪks/
history /'hɪstəri/
geography /dʒi'ɒgrəfi/
spelling /'spelɪŋ/
literature /'lɪtrətʃə(r)/
science /'saɪəns/
biology /baɪ'ɒlədʒi/
religion /rɪ'lɪdʒən/
cookery /'kʊkəri/
art /ɑ:t/
physics /'fɪzɪks/
chemistry /'kemɪstri/
banker /'bæŋkə(r)/
farmer /'fɑ:mə(r)/
journalist /'dʒɜ:nəlɪst/
happiness /'hæpɪnəs/
friendship /'frendʃɪp/
health /helθ/
refund /'ri:fʌnd/

### Verbs

order /'ɔ:də(r)/
switch on /swɪtʃ 'ɒn/
switch off /swɪtʃ 'ɒf/
(It doesn't) work
go (bzzz)
apologize /ə'pɒlədʒaɪz/
replace /ri'pleɪs/
prefer /prɪ'fɜ:(r)/

### Adjectives

useless /'ju:sləs/
necessary /'nesəsri/
busy /'bɪzi/
strange /streɪndʒ/

### Other words and expressions

least /li:st/
That's all right.
I thought you said...
secondly /'sekəndli/
thirdly /'θɜ:dli/
I *do* apologize. /aɪ 'du: ə'pɒlədʒaɪz/
instead /ɪn'sted/

# Unit 31

## Grammar and structures

### Reflexive pronouns

myself /maɪˈself/
yourself /jɔːˈself/
himself /hɪmˈself/
herself /həˈself/
itself /ɪtˈself/
ourselves /aʊəˈselvz/
yourselves /jɔːˈselvz/
themselves /ðəmˈselvz/

Stop looking at **yourself** in the mirror.
'Can I help you?' 'I'll do it **myself**, thanks.'
I like going for walks **by myself**.

### Possessive pronouns

mine /maɪn/
yours /jɔːz/
his /hɪz/
hers /hɜːz/
ours /aʊəz/
theirs /ðeəz/

That's not **yours** – it's **mine**.
Our baby's prettier than **theirs**.

**Whose** is that?

### Indefinite pronouns

| | | | |
|---|---|---|---|
| somebody | anybody | everybody | nobody |
| something | anything | everything | nothing |
| somewhere | anywhere | everywhere | nowhere |

There's **somebody** at the door.
Would you like **anything** to drink?
You can find Coca Cola **everywhere**.
'What are you doing?' '**Nothing**.'

### Shall

**Shall** I carry something for you?
I'll open the door, **shall** I?

### Would

Would you like something to drink?
I'd like some tea.
I prefer coffee.
'Would you like to dance?' 'I'd love to.'

### Else

Do you do the ironing yourself, or does **somebody else** do it for you?
'Would you like **something else**?' 'No, **nothing else**, thank you.'

### Other structures

They talk to **each other** in English.
They've known **each other** for years.

do the ironing    do the cleaning    do the shopping

I've **just** had breakfast.

'Shall I take your coat?' 'No thanks, **I'll keep it on**.'

That's very kind of you.

That car belongs to my boss.

## Words and expressions to learn

### Nouns

the ironing /ði ˈaɪənɪŋ/
the cleaning /ðə ˈkliːnɪŋ/
the washing /ðə ˈwɒʃɪŋ/
the washing-up /ðə wɒʃɪŋ ˈʌp/
the shopping /ðə ˈʃɒpɪŋ/
toast /təʊst/
plate /pleɪt/
argument /ˈɑːgjʊmənt/
mirror /ˈmɪrə(r)/

### Verbs

hurt /hɜːt/ (hurt /hɜːt/, hurt /hɜːt/)
visit /ˈvɪzɪt/
teach /tiːtʃ/ (taught /tɔːt/, taught /tɔːt/)
shall /ʃəl, ʃæl/
carry /ˈkæri/
put on (TV) /pʊt ˈɒn/
keep on (clothes) /kiːp ˈɒn/ (kept /kept/, kept /kept/)
belong (to) /bɪˈlɒŋ tə/
shut /ʃʌt/ (shut /ʃʌt/, shut /ʃʌt/)

### Other words and expressions

about /əˈbaʊt/
else /els/
just /dʒʌst/
just now /dʒʌst ˈnaʊ/
whose /huːz/
awake /əˈweɪk/
anybody /ˈenibɒdi/
anywhere /ˈeniweə(r)/
nowhere /ˈnəʊweə(r)/
shake hands with /ʃeɪk ˈhændz wɪð/
get away from /get əˈweɪ frəm/
have a look /hæv ə ˈlʊk/
have a rest /hæv ə ˈrest/
wash (your) hands /ˈwɒʃ (jɔː) ˈhændz/

THERE IS NO SUMMARY FOR UNIT 32.

# Acknowledgements

The authors and publishers would like to thank the following institutions for their help in testing the material and for the invaluable feedback which they provided:

ILC, Paris, France; Sociedade Brasileira de Cultura Inglesa, Curitiba, Brazil; International Language Centre, Athens, Greece; Adult Migrant Education Service, Australia; Ecole Nationale des Pontes et Chaussées, Paris, France; Communications in Business, Paris, France; Audiovisuelles Sprachinstitut, Zürich, Switzerland; Institut Supérieur de Langues Vivantes, University of Liège, Belgium; Studio School of English, Cambridge; The Cambridge School of English, London; English International, London; International Language Centre, Kuwait; Instituto Anglo-Mexicano de Cultura (Centro and Sur), Mexico; The British Institute of Rome, Italy; Englisches Institut, Köln, West Germany; The Gulf Polytechnic, Bahrain; Institut de Linguistique Appliquée, Strasbourg; Université Lyon 2, France; Abteilung für Angewandte Linguistik, Universität Bern, Switzerland; The British Council, Milan, Italy; International House, Hastings; English Language Centre, Hove, Sussex; Newnham Language Centre, Cambridge; The British Centre, Venice, Italy; Glostrup Pædagogisk Central, Denmark; Kochi Women's University, Kochi-shi, Japan; Institut Français de Gestion, Paris, France; The British Institute, Paris, France; The British School, Florence, Italy; Helmonds Avondcollege, Netherlands; Kodak Pathé, Paris, France; Bell School, Cambridge; Oxford Language Centre, Oxford.

The authors and publishers are grateful to the following copyright owners for permission to reproduce photographs, illustrations, texts and music:

page 26: *tl* The Tate Gallery, London; *c* Reprinted by permission of Ekdotike Athenon, S.A.; *tr* Reprinted by permission of Royal Gallery of Paintings: Mauritshuis; *br* Copyright © Trustees of the British Museum. The excerpt on the cassette from *Eine Kleine Nachtmusik* by Mozart is from a Decca recording and is used with permission. page 29: *bl* Copyright © 1954 by Ronald Searle; *br* Copyright © Associated Newspapers Group plc. page 41: *br* Copyright © 1956 by Ronald Searle. page 51: *t* Ms. Auct. D. inf. 2.11, Folios 3, 7 & 10 recto. By permission of The Bodleian Library, Oxford. page 53: *c, cr* Copyright © Associated Newspapers Group plc; *br* Reproduced by permission of *Punch*. page 61: Reproduced by permission of *Punch*. page 65: *Musical Swag* by Pierre Ranson, Copyright © Tony Bingham. page 80: *tr, bl* Reproduced by permission of *Punch*. page 86: The words of *Why, Oh Why* are copyright © 1960, 1964 and 1972 Ludlow Music Inc. New York, assigned to Tro Essex Music Limited at 85 Gower Street, London WC1. International copyright secured. All rights reserved. Used by permission. page 88: By permission of Rolls-Royce Motors Limited. page 90: *l* Courtesy of the Prado Museum, Madrid; *r* Cliché des Musées Nationaux, Paris. page 96: The lyrics of *Pick it up* are copyright © 1954 Folkways Music Publishers Inc. New York, assigned to Kensington Music Limited at 85 Gower Street, London WC1. International copyright secured. All rights reserved. Used by permission. page 97: *t* copyright © Penguin Books 1973. page 98: *br*, Courtesy of Hilton International, London. page 99: *t* Reproduced by permission of London Transport (Registered User No. 83/200). page 100: *c* Courtesy of British Airways. page 117: *t* Reproduced by permission of *Punch*. page 122: Reproduced by permission of *Punch*. page 126: *ct, tr* By Lucy Bowden. page 130: *t* Copyright © Garsmanda Limited. page 132: *tl, tr, c* Reproduced by permission of *Punch*; *bl* Reproduced by permission of Express Newspapers; *br* From *The Thurber Carnival* by James Thurber. © 1943 James Thurber © 1963 Hamish Hamilton Limited. © 1971 Helen W. Thurber and Rosemary T. Sauers. From *Men, Women and Dogs* published by Harcourt Brace Jovanovich.
  BBC Hulton Picture Library: p63 *cr, br*. Brenard Photo Services Limited: p79. Colorific Photo Library Limited: p7 *no. 4*, p19 *ct*, inset *bl, cr*, p21, p38 *cr*, p63 *cl*, p107 *nos. 1, 3, 5, 6*. Colour Library International (Keystone Press Agency Limited): p7 *no. 3*, p9 *no. 2*, p107 *no. 2*, p109 *c*. Daily Telegraph Colour Library: p19 inset *cl*. The Image Bank of Photography: p66 *Thomas, Mike*, p67 *c B, D, F*, p109 *B, D, E, F*. Alan Philip: p10 *nos. 1-6*, p17, p30 *.*, p35, p50 *r*, p71 *t*, p104 *t*, p115 *t*, p126 *br*. Pictor International Limited: p9 *cr*, p11 *cr*, p14, p66 *Kate, Stuart, Ann*, p67 *A-E, c A, C, E*, p108 *cl, br*, p109 *A*. Scala Istituto Fotografico Editoriale s.p.a: p63 *t*. Sporting Pictures (UK) Limited: p78 Stockphotos International: p66 *Mark*, p107 *no.4*. Tony Stone Associates: p19 *cr*, p108 *tr*. Syndication International Limited: p7 *nos. 1, 5, 7, 8, 9*, p9 *nos. 5, 6*. John Topham Picture Library: p7 *nos. 2, 6, 10*, p9 *nos. 1, 3, 4, 7, 8*, p19 *tl, ct, cb*, inset *tr, br*, p38 *tr*.
  John Craddock: Malcolm Barter, Suzanne Lihou, Alexa Rutherford, Kate Simunek. Ian Fleming and Associates Limited: Terry Burton. Davis Lewis Management: Richard Dunn, Bob Harvey, Barry Thorpe. Linden Artists Limited: David Astin, Jon Davies, Tim Marwood, Val Sangster, Malcolm Stokes, Linda Worrell. Temple Art Agency: Mark Bergin, John James, John Marshall, Alan Philpot, Mike Whittlesea. Richard Baldwin, Richard Child, Kaye Hodges, Chris Rawlings, Malcolm Ward, Mike Woodhatch, Youé and Spooner.

(*t* = top *b* = bottom *c* = centre *r* = right *l* = left)

Note for Spain:
Aprobado por orden Ministerial N. 2531/1974 de 20 de julio (B.O. del E. de 13 de septiembre) y en la Orden de 2 de diciembre de 1974 (B.O. del E. del 16) para 1° de bachillerato. Madrid 19 de noviembre 1984.